Crafts Magazine

Best wishes

gifts for special occasions

CREATIVE PUBLISHING international

MINNETONKA, MINNESOTA

Table of Contents

Weddings

Whether you make a shower gift they can use for their big day, a
wedding present that can store their cherished memories or just
something thoughtful for the couple's new home, these handcrafted
items help celebrate the most special day of their lives.

Wedding Memories Shadow Box

Preserve mementos long after the honeymoon is over with a shadow box filled with tokens from the dream-come-true day. Choose a premade frame; then, with an easy-to-use tool, cut a mat in a color of your choice. Add the mementos shown in our memory box, or choose other favorites for a treasure that will last until the couple's golden anniversary.

List of Materials

- 11″ x 14″ x 1⅝″ (28 x 35.5 x 4 cm) shadow box picture frame, one
- White mat board, 11″ x 14″ (28 x 35.5 cm)
- Oval/circle mat cutter, or purchase a precut white mat board
- ⅛″ (3 mm) white foamcore board, 20″ x 30″ (51 x 76 cm)
- Ice blue floral spray paint
- Repositionable spray adhesive

- Trims: ⅓ yd. (0.32 m) 6″ (15 cm) flat lace; ³⁄₁₆″ (4.5 mm) ribbon: 2¼ yd. (2.1 m) pink satin picot; 4 yd. (3.7 m) gold lamé; 3 mm pink pearl sprays, 12
- Florals: pink silk daisy spray with nine 1½″ (3.8 cm) flowers; 3″ (7.5 cm) silk lily of the valley sprigs, three; silk ivy spray with five 5″ (12.5 cm) sections of ½″ to 1″ (1.3 to 2.5 cm) leaves

- Assorted wedding memorabilia: 5″ x 7″ (12.5 x 18 cm) photo; invitation; garter; rice bag; favor
- 32-gauge white cloth-covered wire
- White floral tape
- Glues: white craft; silicone
- Miscellaneous items: scissors, 18″ (46 cm) metal ruler, craft knife or straight line mat cutter, pencil, wire cutters, transparent tape, glass cleaner, paper towels

1. Using the oval/circle mat cutter, cut a 4¼" x 6¼" (10.8 x 15.7 cm) oval in the mat board center. Use the straight line cutter to cut a 11" x 14" (28 x 35.5 cm) piece of foamcore for the backing. Also cut 4 foamcore spacers to fit the inside walls of the frame; they will stand on 1 edge between the glass and the mat board to produce the shadowbox effect.

2. Refer to the photo for all Steps below. Spray the back of the lace with the adhesive. Refer to the Step 2 illustration to adhere it diagonally across the lower left corner of the mat. Lightly spray ice blue paint over the lace. Let dry. Remove the lace and repeat in the top right corner.

3. Glue the invitation slightly angled to the lower right corner, using raised mounds of silicone glue to lift up the top half. Let dry. Glue the garter at an angle to the lower left corner just below the opening. Glue the rice bag and favor slightly overlapping the garter.

4. Cut two 1 yd. (0.95 m) lengths of gold ribbon and two 2" (5 cm) wires. With each ribbon, form a bow with eight 1½" (3.8 cm) loops and two 6" (15 cm) streamers; wire at the center to secure. Glue the bows side by side between the rice bag and favor. Cut two 5" (12.5 cm) sections from the ivy, then cut into 2- to 3-leaf clusters. Cut the daisies from their stems. Glue 2 daisies between the rice bag and favor, and the ivy around the daisies and between the gold bow loops.

5. Cut two 4" (10 cm) wires. Use the remaining gold ribbon to form a bow with eight 1½" (3.8 cm) loops and two 18" (46 cm) streamers; wire at the center to secure. From the pink ribbon, cut one 1⅔ yd. (1.58 m) length and one 20" (51 cm) length. Use the 1⅔ yd. (1.58 m) ribbon to form a bow with ten 2" (5 cm) loops and two 10" (25.5 cm) streamers; wire at the center to secure. Center and wire the 20" (51 cm) ribbon below the base of the bow for additional streamers. Stack and wire the gold bow on top of the pink bow; trim the excess wire. Glue the layered bow at an angle to the top left, 3" (7.5 cm) from the corner.

6. Glue a 5" (12.5 cm) ivy section on each side of the layered bow to form a crescent, as seen in the Step 6 illustration. Glue a cluster of 3 daisies between the bow loops. Glue 1 daisy and 1 lily of the valley sprig nestled in the ivy on each side of the crescent. Twist and curl the pink and gold streamers out toward the ends of the crescent, spot gluing as necessary.

7. Glue 1 daisy, 1 lily of the valley sprig and several ivy leaves in a cluster above the invitation with the stems tucked behind it. Tape 2 pearl sprays together, then trim the stem to ½" (1.3 cm). Repeat to make 6 double pearl sprays; glue them randomly throughout.

8. Tape the photo centered behind the mat opening. Make sure the glass is clean and free of any dust. With the frame face down, position the glass into the back. Place the spacers along the inside frame walls, then the decorated mat face down resting on the spacers, followed by the foamcore. Secure the edges with the frame push points.

Picture Perfect Frame

Paint a papier-mâché frame shimmering white and embellish it with lace, beads and bows to create a special keepsake for the bride and groom. This frame is made to stand vertically, but it can also stand horizontally. Just follow the instructions working with the frame in a horizontal position.

List of Materials

- 5" x 7" (12.5 x 18 cm) papier-mâché frame with oval opening
- White wash acrylic paint
- Shimmering white fabric paint
- No. 8 round brush

- ½" (1.3 cm) scalloped white lace, ½ yd. (0.5 m)
- 1" (2.5 cm) premade white bows with ribbon rose centers, two
- ⅛" (3 mm) white satin cord, ¾ yd. (0.7 m)

- 5 mm white pearl beads, approximately 130
- White craft glue
- Miscellaneous items: scissors, disposable palette, tweezers

Paint the front and back of the frame with 2 coats of white wash, letting the paint dry between coats.

Glue the halfway point of the lace to the top center of the oval frame opening. See the Step 2 illustration to continue gluing the lace around each side of the opening, trimming the ends of the lace where they meet at the center bottom. Glue a bow to cover the cut ends of the lace.

Begin at the top center frame edge to glue the satin cord around the outer frame edge. Be careful not to glue the cord over the opening for the photo at the top of the frame. Glue a bow to cover the cut ends of the cord. Let glue dry.

Paint the entire front and back of the frame, including the lace, cording and bows, with shimmering white fabric paint, using a dabbing motion with the paintbrush to work the paint into all the crevices. Let dry.

To glue each bead to the lace, squeeze a puddle of glue onto a disposable palette. Using the tweezers, dip each bead into glue and place on the lace, as shown in the Step 5 illustration. Follow the pattern of the lace to glue the beads in a symmetrical design on the lace. Let glue dry.

Woven Ribbon Ring Pillow

A handmade pillow is the perfect way to carry treasured wedding rings to the altar. The hexagon pattern for this pillow top is formed by weaving satin ribbons in three directions. Weave white and ivory ribbons for this classic look, or choose ribbon colors to match the wedding colors.

List of Materials

- Ribbons: 1/8″ (3 mm) white satin, 1 1/2 yd. (1.4 m); 3/8″ (1 cm): white satin (A), cream satin (B), white floral satin (C), 5 1/2 yd. (5.05 m) each; white/gold satin, 1/2 yd. (0.5 m); 7/8″ (2.2 cm) wire-edge: sheer white/gold novelty, 1/2 yd. (0.5 m); white/gold taffeta, 1/3 yd. (0.32 m)
- Fusible interfacing, 9″ (23 cm) square
- White satin fabric for backing, 9″ (23 cm) square
- Polyester fiberfill

- Hot glue gun
- Potpourri (optional)
- Pattern Page 164
- Miscellaneous items: yardstick or tape measure, scissors, wire cutters, sewing machine, sewing needle, matching thread, iron, straight pins, blunt needle, 9″ (23 cm) square heavyweight cardboard, press cloth, tracing paper, pencil

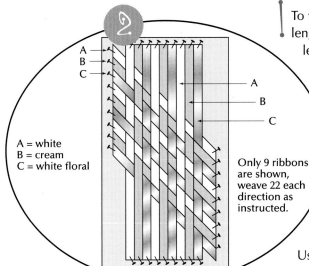

A = white
B = cream
C = white floral

Only 9 ribbons are shown, weave 22 each direction as instructed.

1 To weave the fabric for the pillow top, cut twenty-two 9″ (23 cm) lengths each of Ribbons A, B and C. Letters correspond to the letters in the Materials Box. Center the fusible interfacing on the cardboard, fusible side up.

2 Alternating Ribbons A, B and C, pin 22 vertical ribbons, side by side with ribbons touching but not overlapping, to the cardboard over the interfacing. See the Step 2 illustration to weave the first set of 22 diagonal ribbons from left to right as follows, beginning in the upper left corner:

Ribbon A: under A and C, and over B.
Ribbon B: under A and B, and over C.
Ribbon C: under B and C, and over A.

Use a blunt needle to gently lift ribbons as you weave under them.

3 To weave the second set of 22 diagonal ribbons, begin in the lower left corner. Alternate Ribbons A, B and C, weaving diagonally from left to right, to make hexagon shapes as follows:

Ribbon A: under vertical C and diagonal C; over vertical A and B; under diagonal A; repeat.
Ribbon B: under vertical A and diagonal A; over vertical B and C; under diagonal B; repeat.
Ribbon C: under vertical B and diagonal B; over vertical C and A; under diagonal C; repeat.

4 After weaving all ribbons, straighten and line them up evenly, if necessary, and pin at each end. Place a damp press cloth over the woven ribbon fabric and refer to the manufacturer's instructions to fuse the fabric to the interfacing. For the pillow backing, trace the heart pattern and cut from satin fabric.

5 Use a pencil to trace the heart pattern onto the interfacing side of the woven fabric. Position the pattern so that the hexagon "cubes" on the fabric will be right-side-up on the heart. Machine-stitch short stitches along the traced line. Cut out the heart close to the stitching line.

6 Baste each end of the 3/8″ (1 cm) white/gold satin ribbon to the top edge of the heart for a hanging loop; see the Step 6 illustration. Sew the pillow, right sides together, using a 1/4″ (6 mm) seam, leaving an opening for turning. Clip corners and turn. Stuff pillow lightly with fiberfill and, if desired, with potpourri. Slipstitch the opening closed.

7 To trim the heart, refer to the photo. Use the 7/8″ (2.2 cm) sheer novelty ribbon to tie a 2-loop bow with streamers. Use the 1/8″ (3 mm) white satin ribbon to form a 6-loop bow with 4 streamers. Wire the center of the bow to secure, then wire it to the center of the 2-loop bow. Knot the 1/8″ (3 mm) streamer ends. Glue the wired bows to the center top of the heart. Tie the rings to 2 of the 1/8″ (3 mm) streamers.

8 For the ribbon rose, tie a knot at 1 end of the gold/white taffeta wire-edge ribbon. On the opposite end, poke out a wire end from 1 edge. Loosely gather ribbon along this wire to the knot. Do not trim the wire. Holding the knot in one hand, spiral the gathered ribbon loosely around the knot to form the rose. At the end, fold under the raw edge and secure by wrapping the wire tightly around the knot. Trim the wire end. Glue the ribbon rose to the center of the wired bows.

Floral Fantasy Guest Album

Only four simple embroidery stitches are used in this heart full of ribbon flowers done on a square of satin. Pad, and then glue the stitched design to the front of the album of your choice, finish the edges easily with a string of pearl beads, and you have a unique handmade gift for the married couple that they will treasure, along with the memories it holds, their whole lives.

List of Materials

- 6" x 8" (15 x 20.5 cm) white fabric-covered guest book
- Pale pink or white satin, 6" (15 cm) square
- Embroidery floss: cream; light green; pale pink
- 4 mm embroidery ribbon: pale pink, 5 yd. (4.6 m); cream, 4 yd.

(3.7 m), soft aqua, 3 yd. (2.75 m); pale green, 6 yd. (5.5 m)

- Embroidery needle
- Trims: 4 mm white fused pearls, 1/2 yd. (0.5 m); 5/8" (1.5 cm) pale pink wire-edge ribbon, 1/3 yd. (0.32 m); 1/8" (3 mm) cream satin ribbon, 3/4 yd. (0.7 m)

- Low-loft batting, 6" (15 cm) square
- Glues: thick white craft; hot glue gun
- Miscellaneous items: tracing paper, dressmaker's carbon, pencil, scissors, 6" (15 cm) square lightweight cardboard, embroidery hoop (optional)

1 Refer to the Ribbon Embroidery Stitches on page 159 to stitch the design. Trace the Ribbon Embroidery Guide and transfer to center front of satin square.

2 Use green ribbon to stitch lazy daisy leaves and aqua to work single wrap French knots. Work spider web roses using 2 strands of pink or cream floss for the spokes and matching ribbon for the roses. Work stem stitches for stems using 3 strands of green floss.

3 Trace the heart pattern and cut out as indicated. Glue batting to front of cardboard heart. Center finished embroidery on padded heart. Wrap and glue excess fabric to back, trimming and clipping curves as needed.

4 Hot-glue padded heart to center front of guest book. Glue pearl string around heart edges. Tie wire-edge ribbon and two 12" (30.5 cm) lengths of 1/8" (3 mm) ribbon together in a bow. Refer to the photo to glue to front binding.

Ribbon Embroidery Guide & Heart Pattern

Cut 1 each from batting and cardboard
1 of 1

Floral Fantasy Guest Album
Color/Stitch Key

Stitch	Color
✎ Lazy Daisy Leaf	Green Ribbon
✪ Spider Web Rose	Pink Floss & Ribbon
Spider Web Rose	Cream Floss & Ribbon
● French Knot	Aqua Ribbon
＼ Stem Stitch	Green Floss

Roses & Romance Cardholder

Make sure that guest cards don't get lost at the reception with much more than a paper-covered box. Create a wonderful garden-inspired wedding accessory using ivory roses, lily of the valley and ivy on a birdcage. A hint of gold sponged on the background and golden berry sprigs add an elegant touch to the natural beauty of the design.

List of Materials

- Ivory wicker birdcage, 8″ x 8″ x 15″ (20.5 x 20.5 x 38 cm)
- 8″ (20.5 cm) gold lamé fabric squares, two
- Cardboard square, 8″ (20.5 cm)
- Spray adhesive
- Floral color sprays: walnut wood tone; metallic gold
- Green silk ivy sprays with four

6″ (15 cm) sections of ¹/₂″ to 1¹/₂″ (1.3 to 3.8 cm) leaves, three
- Ivory silk rose sprays with one 1¹/₂″ (3.8 cm) and one 3″ (7.5 cm) open rose and two ¹/₂″ (1.3 cm) buds, four
- Ivory silk lily of the valley picks with four 3¹/₂″ (9 cm) flower sections, eight

- 17″ (43 cm) gold artificial berry spray, one
- Gold painted forked twigs, 4″ to 6″ (10 to 15 cm), four
- ³/₄″ (2 cm) metallic gold chiffon ribbon, 2 yd. (1.85 m)
- 32-gauge cloth-covered wire
- Miscellaneous items: ruler, scissors, hot glue gun, wire cutters, small piece of sponge

1. Refer to the manufacturer's instructions to adhere fabric with spray adhesive to both sides of the cardboard square. Glue the square to the bottom of the birdcage. Cut off the horizontal center bar support from 3-4 bars, to make an opening for the cards.

2. Lightly mist the ivy leaves with the wood tone spray. Let dry between colors and each step. Spray metallic gold onto a slightly damp sponge. Sponge the color on the cage, allowing the ivory to show through in places.

3. Leaving 1/2" (1.3 cm) stems, cut the ivy leaves, roses and lily of the valley from their main stems. Refer to the photo and the Step 3 illustration to glue ivy leaves around the base and one 3" (7.5 cm) rose at each bottom corner of the birdcage. Glue 28 lily of the valley flowers between the ivy leaves. Randomly glue 3 rosebuds between the ivy leaves and lily of the valley.

4. From the berry stem, cut five 2" (5 cm) lengths, each with a cluster of 3 berries. Glue 1 cluster above the rose at each bottom corner of the cage.

5. To decorate the top of the cage, glue a cluster of 2 lily of the valley leaves, one 1 1/2" (3.8 cm) rose, 1 bud and 4 lily of the valley sections just in front and to 1 side of the hanging loop. Fill in with ivy leaves around the cluster. Add 1 berry cluster and the gold painted twigs.

6. Tie the chiffon ribbon into a bow with six 1 1/2" (3.8 cm) loops and two 12" (30.5 cm) streamers; secure the center with wire. Also cut one 8" (20.5 cm), 12" (30.5 cm) and 15" (38 cm) length of ribbon for streamers. Glue the streamers, then the bow to the top of the cage behind the flower cluster, allowing the ends to cascade down the sides. Cut a "V" in each streamer end.

Toasting Glasses

Whether the glasses are filled with juice, water or bubbly champagne, an integral part of almost any wedding reception is the toast, complete with a speech from the best man. How much more special this tradition is with handmade glasses. Do the flutes as shown (with "Bride" and "Groom"), or personalize them by using their first names. Change the roses to a meaningful decorative design, such as a sailboat for mariner types or leaves for an autumn wedding.

List of Materials

- 2 champagne flutes
- Roses stencil*
- Plaid® Fun to Paint™ Tip-Pen Craft Tip Set™*
- Glass etching creme*
- Stencil adhesive spray

- Empty 2 oz. acrylic craft paint bottle
- Practice glass surface, such as a jar
- 1/2" (1.3 cm) or narrower masking tape

- Miscellaneous items: scrap paper, pencil

*(See Sources on page 175 for purchasing information.)

1 Purchase an empty 2 oz. (59 mL) paint bottle, or remove the flip-top lid and empty out a paint bottle into a bowl. Cover the bowl with plastic wrap so you can pour it back in the bottle later. Make sure to check that the Plaid nozzle from the Craft Tip Set will fit your paint bottle; if it is a Plaid paint bottle it will fit for sure. Wash out the paint bottle, and let dry. Fill 1/3 full of etching creme. Put the plastic nozzle and the extra-fine tip on the bottle.

2 Practice writing Bride and Groom on scratch paper with a pencil to get a size that will fit well on the glasses and a style you like and are comfortable writing. This can be either script or printing. Remember, you may choose to use the happy couple's first names instead of Bride and Groom.

3 Use the etching creme to write the words you practiced in Step 2 on your glass jar or other practice glass surface. Try to use a practice surface that is about as curvy as the champagne flutes, because working on a curved surface is different than working on a flat surface. Notice how fast the etching creme flows through the tip, and how quickly or slowly you must work.

4 Follow the manufacturer's instructions for how long to leave the etching creme on; EtchAll® requires 15 minutes. Rinse off the etching creme thoroughly in a sink and completely down the drain. Dry the glass to reveal your work. Practice a few more times until you are satisfied with the results.

5 See the Step 5 illustration to place a strip of masking tape on each flute at approximately the same angle. Angling the words allows them to be seen without rotating the glass; this is important when using a narrow flute. The tape will be a guide only; the etching creme should not come in contact with the tape. Write the words Bride or Groom about 1/4" (6 mm) above the tape edge on either flute, just as you practiced in Step 3. After the required length of time, wash away the etching creme as in Step 4.

6 Cut out a rose motif from the stencil for the Bride's flute, and another for the Groom's. Follow the stencil adhesive manufacturer's instructions to spray the back of the stencil with adhesive and, when ready, place the stencil on the appropriate flute to the right of and below the words. Put masking tape around the edges to prevent any creme escaping from the desired areas. Continue to use the extra-fine tip applicator to "draw" inside the stencil images, and fill them in solidly with etching creme.

7 Allow the creme to process for the required time, then wash off the etching creme over the sink. When all is clean, remove the stencil. Touch up any of the etched motifs, if necessary, by adding more etching creme with the applicator tip or a paint-brush. Allow the creme to process, and clean up as in Step 4. Add other decorative designs all around the glass or on the base, if desired, following Steps 6 and 7.

Cross-Stitch Album Cover

Clusters of calla lilies frame this exquisite cross-stitch wedding sampler. A twist on the traditional wedding sampler, this elegant design is mounted on the front of a wedding album and framed in gimp braid. It will hold wonderful remembrances of a special day to last a lifetime.

List of Materials

- 26-count gold lurex evenweave fabric, 12" x 14" (30.5 x 35.5 cm)
- 6-strand skeins of embroidery floss in colors listed in Color Key
- Metallic gold (002HL) No. 8 fine braid
- No. 24 tapestry needle

- 10" x 11½" (25.5 x 29.3 cm) white photo album
- Double-face sheet adhesive for crafts, 12" x 14" (30.5 x 35.5 cm)
- ⅝" (1.5 cm) white gimp braid, 1½ yd. (1.4 m)
- 1" (2.5 cm) white ribbon rose, one

- ⅛" (3 mm) white satin ribbon, 1 yd. (0.95 m)
- Hot glue gun or white craft glue
- Pattern Page 162
- Miscellaneous items: scissors, ruler

1 Refer to the Album Cover Stitch Chart on page 162 to stitch the design over 2 threads of the evenweave fabric. Symbols on the chart correspond to colors on the Color Key. Each square represents 2 threads of evenweave fabric.

2 Use the Alphabet/Numbers Chart below to stitch the names and date where indicated on the Album Cover Chart, centering each line.

3 Refer to the Cross-Stitch General Instructions and Stitches on page 160 to work all cross-stitches with 2 strands of floss or 1 strand of metallic braid, and all backstitches with 1 strand of floss. Use dark antique blue (1035) for the words and medium gray (400) for all other backstitches.

4 Follow the manufacturer's instructions to apply the sheet adhesive to the wrong side of the stitched piece. Keeping the design centered, trim the fabric to 8³/4" x 10¹/4" (22.4 x 26 cm). Remove the paper backing and center the stitched design on the front of the album.

5 Beginning at the top left corner, glue the gimp braid around the fabric edges, mitering the corners. Cut the satin ribbon in half. Align the ends and fold the ribbons in half. Glue the folded edges to the top left corner over the braid, with 1 pair of streamers extending down and the other pair extending horizontally to the right. Glue the 1" (2.5 cm) ribbon rose over the folded ribbons in the corner. Arrange the ribbon streamers to fall in soft curves down the side and across the top; spot glue in place.

Alphabet/Numbers Stitch Chart 1 of 2

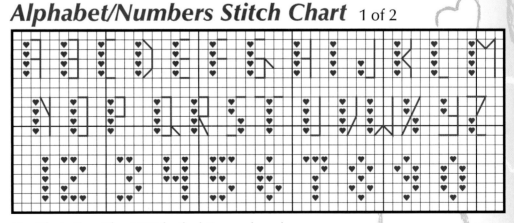

Use Dk. Antique Blue 1035 for the letters and numbers.
The Album Cover Chart is on page 162.

Romantic Hurricane Globe

The glimmer of candlelight becomes even more romantic flickering amongst the lilacs and roses on this painted hurricane globe. A gorgeous accent for the wedding ceremony or reception, the bride and groom will continue to enjoy its beauty in their home for years to come.

List of Materials

- 14" to 16" (35.5 to 40.5 cm) clear glass hurricane globe
- Self-adhesive paper-backed vinyl sheet, 8¹/₂" x 11" (21.8 x 28 cm)
- Glass and tile medium
- Acrylic paints: wicker white; berry wine; violet pansy; Hauser dark green; Hauser light green
- Paintbrushes: No. 12 flat; No. 4 scrubber; No. 1 script liner
- Pattern Page 163
- Miscellaneous items: tracing paper, pencil, scissors, masking tape, white vinegar, soft cloth, disposable palette, water basin, paper towels

1. To prepare the globe, use a soft cloth to wash it with a mixture of 3 parts water to 1 part vinegar. Let dry.

2. Trace the pattern from Pattern Page 163. Cut the heart from the self-adhesive vinyl to make a masking template. Remove the paper backing and refer to the photo to adhere the masking template to the globe just above the center.

3. To "frost" the glass, refer to the manu-facturer's instructions to apply the glass and tile medium to the outside of the globe. Let dry for 24 hours.

4. Remove the masking template. To paint the design, refer to the photo and the Painting Instructions and Techniques on page 156. Let dry between paint colors and each step unless otherwise indicated. Double load the No. 12 brush with wicker white and berry wine and paint the inner and outer heart edges using S strokes as shown in the Step 4 illustration.

5. To paint the floral design, tape the pattern to the inside of the globe. Double load the brush with wicker white and berry wine to paint the center rose and the rosebuds. Double load the brush with Hauser light green and Hauser dark green and combine left-angle and right-angle S strokes to paint the leaves, painting with the light color at the top of the leaf.

6. See the Step 6 illustration to use a stippling motion of the scrubber brush to paint the baby's breath with violet pansy. While wet, add wicker white to the brush and stipple over the top of the violet pansy.

7. Thin Hauser light green with water to an inky consistency and use the script liner to paint curlicues. Let dry for 3 hours.

8. Apply 2 coats of glass and tile medium over the painted design, letting dry between coats. To light, use a pillar candle or a candlestick lamp. Use of a taper candle is not recommended. Never leave a lit candle unattended.

Handmade Wedding Cards

Make elegant cards to express your best wishes to the bride and groom and identify your gift for the happy pair. The cards are made simply by embossing and pin punching watercolor paper, then embellishing them with assorted lace and ribbons.

List of materials

- 140-pound watercolor paper
- 3/8" (1 cm) white satin ribbon/silver edge, 1 yd. (0.95 m)
- White lace: 1 5/8" (4 cm) for card, 3" (7.5 cm); 7/8" (2.2 cm) for gift card, 2" (5 cm)
- Embossing tool

- White craft glue
- Pattern Page 165
- Miscellaneous items: tracing paper, pencil, craft knife, metal edge ruler, straight pin, heavy cardboard, thimble, batting, colored plastic folder, light table (optional)

1 Cut one 5¹/₂″ x 12³/₄″ (14 x 32.4 cm) wedding card and one 3″ x 9″ (7.5 x 23 cm) gift tag. To cut, measure and mark lightly with pencil and ruler. Working on heavy cardboard, place ruler on pencil line and cut along edge with knife. Fold paper with the grain for a clean crease; grainline should run along short side.

2 Using pencil and ruler, divide length of card into three 4¹/₄″ (10.8 cm) sections and gift tag into three 3″ (7.5 cm) sections. Fold at lines and crease inward.

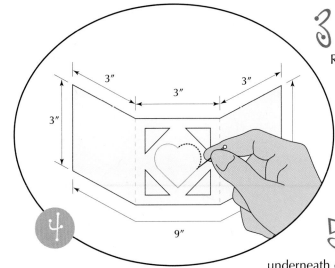

3 Trace the patterns onto tracing paper. Lay tracing facedown on inside center section of each card. Retrace lines with pencil to transfer. All embossing and cutting will be done on penciled lines.

4 Place several layers of batting between card and heavy cardboard work surface. Use straight pin to pierce holes around dotted pattern lines, as shown in the Step 4 illustration.

5 To emboss solid pattern lines, use light table or work against bright window. Place colored folder underneath outside edge of shape to be embossed and ruler along same edge on top of card. Press embossing tool along ruler edge to emboss all solid lines.

6 Using ruler and knife, cut through all dashed pattern lines. On gift tag, cut only to dots at corners.

7 Refer to the photo and the Step 7 illustration to insert ribbon and lace through cut lines, with ends extending ¹/₄″ (6 mm) at back; glue. On gift tag, insert lace first, then ribbon on top. Tie remaining ribbon in small bow, trim ends and glue to center lace heart on card.

8 Glue right section of card onto back of embossed section to cover.

An Ornament for the Newlyweds

If you know a couple who is tying the knot, then this ornament is for them. A few colors of polymer clay and you're in business—just shape and bake! It's guaranteed to be one of those special gifts the couple will always cherish for many Christmases to come.

List of Materials

- Polymer clay: black; white; red; yellow; china doll
- Waterbase gloss sealer
- Acrylic paints: black; white; red
- Paintbrushes: liner; medium flat
- Clay gun with spaghetti disk or garlic press
- Miscellaneous items: aluminum foil, cookie sheet, palette knife, disposable palette, water container, toothpicks, paper clip, wire cutters

1 Refer to the photo throughout for all the steps below. Form the clay figures on a foil-covered cookie sheet. To make the groom's body, mix a small amount of black with white clay to make gray. Roll two 1 3/8" (3.5 cm) gray logs for the pants. Roll two 1/2" x 3/4" (1.3 x 2 cm) black ovals for the shoes and attach them to the bottom of the pant legs. For the torso, form a 1/2" x 3/4" (1.3 x 2 cm) black rectangle and attach it to the top of the pants. For the tuxedo lapels, roll two 3/4" (2 cm) diameter black logs and shape them into wide Vs. Position the lapels pointing outward on the body front. For the tuxedo tail, roll a 3/4" (2 cm) black teardrop. Attach it along the left pant leg with the point of the teardrop even with the pants top. For the shirt ruffle, roll a very thin 1" (2.5 cm) long white log. Place it between the lapels, shaping it into a squiggly line.

2

2 1/8"

Pleats

With white clay, form a half-bell shape. Use the palette knife to indent 2 equally spaced pleats on the dress front. Attach the dress to the groom.

1 1/4"

2 To make the bride's dress, see the Step 2 illustration. For the shoes, roll 2 white 1/4" (6 mm) balls and attach them at the left edge of the dress bottom. For the bodice, form a very thin 1/4" x 3/8" (6 mm x 1 cm) white rectangle and attach it across the dress top.

3 Roll red clay to a 1/8" (3 mm) thickness. Cut a 3/4" x 1 1/8" (2 x 2.8 cm) heart. Place the heart over their waists.

4 For the arms, roll a 1/4" x 1 1/4" (6 mm x 3.2 cm) log each of black and white clay. Attach the black arm to the side of the groom and the white arm to the side of the bride. Turn up 3/8" (1 cm) on the bottom of each arm and attach it to the side of the heart. For the hands, roll two 3/16" (4.5 mm) china doll balls and attach them to the ends of the arms.

5 For the heads, roll two 1/2" (1.3 cm) china doll balls. Attach 1 head to each neck with the sides touching. For the noses, roll 2 tiny china doll balls and attach in the center. To make the hair, use the clay gun to extrude yellow clay through the spaghetti disk, or squeeze clay through a garlic press. Cut and attach 1/2" (1.3 cm) strands to each head.

6 For the groom's top hat, roll black clay to a 1/8" (3 mm) thickness and cut out a 5/8" (1.5 cm) triangle. Attach 1 pointed end to the center top back of the groom's head for the hat crown. For the brim, roll a 5/8" (1.5 cm) black log and attach it to the top of the head in front of the triangle.

7 For the bride's veil, shape a 3/4" x 1 3/4" (2 x 4.5 cm) white triangle. To form, see the Step 7 illustration. Attach the top of the veil to the bride's head. Flatten a 3/16" (4.5 mm) white ball and attach to the top of the head, covering the point of the veil. Use the toothpick point to indent dots around the headpiece circle and along the bottom of the veil and dress. Also indent dots in a half circle on the bodice.

7

Pleats

Curve the pointed end of the triangle to the left. Cut the wide end into 3 staggered tiers, then indent the pleats.

Cut

3/4"

8 To make the hanger, cut a paper clip in half. Insert the cut ends of a U-shaped half into the top of the ornament. Bake the ornament in a 265°F (130°C) oven for 30 to 45 minutes. Let cool completely.

9 Paint the mouths and cheeks red. Let dry between paint coats, colors and each step. Paint each eye white with a black pupil, placed so the couple is looking at each other. Outline the eyes and eyelashes with black. Dot a tiny white highlight in each pupil. Paint 3 vertical black pinstripes on each pant leg. Paint white dashed lines around the heart. If desired, paint the couple's names and/or wedding date on the heart. Brush the entire ornament with gloss sealer; let dry.

Soothing Scents Bath Oil

Life in the fast lane can be challenging at times. A "just for me" retreat can be important to maintaining a loving attitude, even for newlyweds. Add comfort to their lives with a floral bath and body oil to use for massaging weary muscles or to add to a steaming tub of bath water. Lavender and rose essential oils provide the calming effect in this recipe. In place of these, ylang-ylang, apricot and vanilla may also be used.

List of Materials

- Decorative glass bottle with cork, 5" (12.5 cm) tall and opening large enough for flower heads to fit through
- Assorted dried flower heads, your choice, approximately 12 pieces: globe amaranth; lavender; larkspur
- Dried mini rosebuds, approximately 40

- Spanish moss
- 3/8" (1 cm) sheer ribbon, two coordinating shades of pink, 2/3 yd. (0.63 m) each
- Almond oil*, 8 oz. (237 mL)
- Essential oils*: lavender, 12 drops; rose, 4 drops
- Vitamin E oil*, 8 drops
- Paraffin wax

- 28-gauge cloth-covered wire, 3" (7.5 cm)
- Hot glue gun
- Miscellaneous items: scissors, ruler, wire cutters, glass measuring cup, wood spoon, double boiler, empty coffee can (optional)

*(See Sources on pg. 175 for purchasing information.)

1 Wash bottle and dry thoroughly. Place dried flower heads inside the bottle. Mix all oils in glass measuring cup. Pour mixture into bottle and insert cork firmly.

2 Melt paraffin wax in double boiler. If desired, place wax in coffee can, then place can in pan filled with water. Dip cork and top of bottle into melted wax; let harden, as shown in the Step 2 illustration. Repeat dipping until a thick seal forms.

3 To decorate the bottle, glue Spanish moss around neck of bottle. Layer sheer ribbon to make a small multi-loop bow with 6" (15 cm) streamers; use cloth-covered wire to secure bow center.

4 Hot-glue bow to center front of bottle top, nestling it in moss. Refer to the photo to twist bow streamers in pairs (1 of each color), and spot glue to bottle front. Glue a cluster of 3 rosebuds to cover 1 "tacked" spot on each streamer. Glue clusters asymmetrically.

5 Refer to the photo to glue remaining rosebuds to form wide ring around bottle neck.

Delft Blues Embroidered Table Linens

There's nothing like a handmade heirloom gift to say "Best Wishes" to the bride and groom. But with only four easy embroidery stitches, using a plain tablecloth and napkins, you won't break the bank or need a year of advance preparation to make it. It will be the perfect backdrop to the joys of entertaining crowds as a new twosome or for a romantic candlelight dinner.

List of Materials

- 52″ (132 cm) square off-white fabric tablecloth
- Coordinating fabric napkins
- Embroidery floss: dark delft

(798); medium delft (799); light baby blue (3325)
- Embroidery needle
- Iron-on transfer pencil

- Miscellaneous items: tracing paper, iron, tape measure, embroidery hoop, scissors

1 Trace the patterns using the iron-on transfer pencil. Follow the manufacturer's instructions to iron the patterns onto the tablecloth and napkins. Position the tablecloth pattern about 18" (46 cm) from each corner and the napkin pattern about 4" (10 cm) from 1 corner of each napkin, or as desired to fit your table.

2 Place the fabric in the embroidery hoop. Refer to Embroidery Stitches on page 159 and to the pattern and Color/Stitch Key to work all embroidery stitches using 2 strands of floss.

Delft Blues Embroidered Table Linens Color/Stitch Key

Symbol	DMC #	Color/Stitch
	798	Dk. Delft Straight Stitches
	798	Dk. Delft Stem Stitches
	799	Med. Delft Stem Stitches
•	799	Med. Delft French Knot
	799	Med. Delft Satin Stitches
	3325	Lt. Baby Blue Satin Stitches

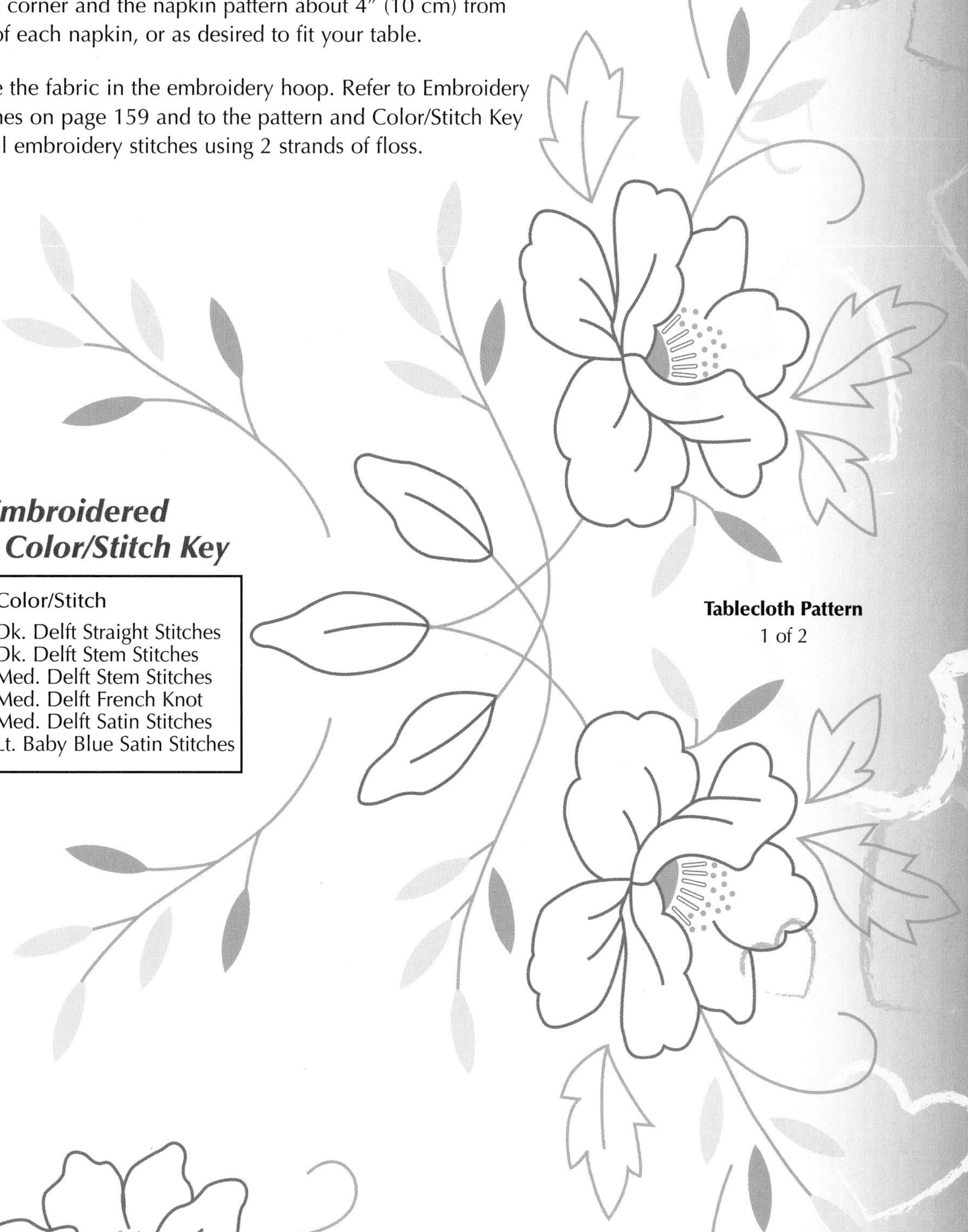

Tablecloth Pattern
1 of 2

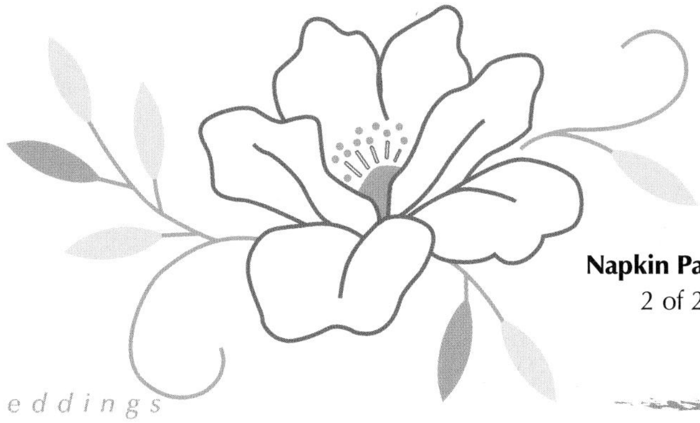

Napkin Pattern
2 of 2

Homespun Casserole Tote

This casserole carrier will please the couple that likes to gather with friends and family for home-cooked meals, picnics and potlucks. Stitched here in cottons and country prints, this could be done up in a rich contemporary tapestry or a cute fuzzy flannel for a totally different look. Whichever style you choose, this homemade wedding gift is guaranteed to get used.

List of Materials

- 45" (115 cm) fabrics: red/white sunflower cotton blend print; red solid quilted, 1 yd. (0.95 m) each
- 45" (115 cm) quilt batting, 1/2 yd. (0.5 m)
- 1 1/2" (3.8 cm) belting, 1 yd. (0.95 m)
- 3/4" (2 cm) Velcro®, 3 1/2" (9 cm) strips, two
- 12" (30.5 cm) wood spoons, two

- 1 1/2" (3.8 cm) wood apples, two
- 1/4" (6 mm) plywood, 9 1/2" (24.3 cm) square
- Glues: fabric, hot glue gun
- Miscellaneous items: scissors, tape measure, sewing machine and matching threads, hand sewing needle, straight pins, drill with bit, iron

1 For the casserole carrier, cut the following 12" x 33" (30.5 x 84 cm) rectangles: sunflower print, 2; red quilted, 2; quilt batting, 1. For the pockets, cut 2 each 8" (20.5 cm) squares from sunflower print and quilted fabric. In the steps that follow, sew all fabrics right sides together, using a 1/2" (1.3 cm) seam allowance unless otherwise indicated. Trim seams and clip curves. After an opening has been left for turning, turn it to the right side, press, and slipstitch the opening closed.

2 To make each pocket, sew together one 8" (20.5 cm) square of sunflower and quilted fabrics, leaving a 2" (5 cm) opening for turning. See the Step 2 illustration to center the finished pockets, print side up, on 1 quilted fabric rectangle. Sew the pockets on 3 sides, leaving the outer edge open. Sew a 1" (2.5 cm) "spoon pocket" on the right side of each pocket.

Leave end open

Raw edges

Spoon pocket   1/2"

3 To make the carrier handle loops, cut four 3 1/2" x 6" (9 x 15 cm) pieces of the sunflower print. Fold each piece in half lengthwise and sew with a 3/8" (1 cm) seam, forming a tube. Turn to the right side and press with seam in center back. Cut four 6" (15 cm) strips of belting and insert 1 in each tube. Fold and pin the tube in half aligning short ends. See the Step 2 illustration to pin loops to the rectangle ends with raw edges extending 1/2" (1.3 cm). Double sew the loops 5/8" (1.5 cm) from loop ends.

4 Align 1 sunflower rectangle on top of pocket rectangle. Sew around edges, leaving 4" (10 cm) open along 1 long edge for turning. Layer the remaining rectangles as follows: batting, sunflower print right side up and quilted piece. Sew around the edges, leaving a 4" (10 cm) opening for turning. Sew the hook side of the Velcro strips onto the quilted side of the rectangle parallel to long edges, 1" (2.5 cm) from each corner. Repeat to sew the loop side of the Velcro strips on the opposite end of the sunflower print.

5 See the Step 5 illustration to criss-cross the rectangles. Sew rectangles together around 3 sides of center square to form pocket for hot dish pad. To make the hot dish pad, cut a 10 1/2" x 21" (26.8 x 53.5 cm) sunflower print rectangle. Fold in half aligning short ends. Sew along 2 opposite sides, leaving the end open; turn. Insert the plywood. Fold the raw edges inward; adhere the edges with fabric glue. Insert the pad into the pocket to reinforce the bottom.

Place the rectangle without pockets on top of

Leave end open

the rectangle with pockets

6 To make each spoon handle, drill a hole in the center top of the apple to fit the spoon handle. Insert the spoon through the loops on the ends of the casserole carrier and insert end of handle into hole in apple.

7 To make 2 pot holders, cut two 6" x 11" (15 x 28 cm) rectangles each from sunflower print and the quilted fabric. Round all 4 corners of each rectangle. To make an end pocket, cut 1 print rectangle and 1 quilted rectangle in half crosswise. Sew print halves to quilt halves along the cut side only. Turn and press. Align the print and quilt fabric rectangles. Sandwich the cut rectangle between the fabric layers with the ends even. Print sides face the same direction. Sew together, leaving a 2" (5 cm) opening for turning. Topstitch around the perimeter of the pot holder. Insert the pot holders in the pockets of the carrier.

Mosaic Trivet & Coasters

The new couple will be able to entertain in style and at the same time protect their furniture with these marvelous mixed media coasters and trivet. Mini ceramic tiles and flat glass marbles form the basic designs, then tile chips and bits of a broken plate fit in the remaining spaces like pieces of a jigsaw puzzle. No patterns are used so each finished mosaic piece is a unique work of art—no two are ever exactly the same.

List of Materials

- Microwaveable plaster
- Mosaic molds: square coaster; round coaster; octagonal trivet
- 3/4" (2 cm) square mosaic ceramic tiles: yellow; green; light blue; royal blue
- Blue pattern china plate—check garage sales and flea markets for chipped dishes to use

- Clear flat glass marbles: blue; amethyst; pink
- Tile nippers
- Mosaic tile adhesive
- White grout
- Glossy white acrylic enamel paint
- 9" x 12" (23 x 30.5 cm) white felt, two sheets

- Rubber feet for trivet, four
- Miscellaneous items: sandpaper, safety goggles, rubber mallet or hammer, newspapers, small disposable plastic container, craft stick, disposable gloves, sponge, small paintbrush, disposable palette, pencil, scissors, white craft glue

1 | Follow the manufacturer's instructions to mix the plaster and mold 2 square coasters, 2 round coasters and 1 octagonal trivet. When thoroughly dry, lightly sand the rough edges.

2 | Refer to the photo to plan your designs. Use the tile nippers to cut some tiles into small triangles, squares and irregular shapes for filling in areas of the designs. To break the plate, place it between layers of newspapers and, wearing safety goggles, use a rubber mallet or hammer to smash the plate into smaller pieces. Use the nippers to cut exact shapes as needed.

3 | Using the large- and medium-size pieces, lay out the pieces in a pleasing combination of colors and shapes on the mold before transferring to the actual plaster surface. Save the smaller pieces to fill in the spaces later.

4 | Apply mosaic glue to a section of the plaster surface and begin transferring the tile design, as shown in the Step 4 illustration. Begin with the center, then the outer edges, and finish by filling in the design. Let dry thoroughly.

5 | Follow the manufacturer's instructions to mix the grout with a craft stick in a small disposable container. Use the stick to spread grout on top of the mosaic surface, filling in all of the cracks. Wearing a disposable plastic glove, smooth over the piece by hand, wiping away the excess grout and smoothing the edges. Let set for 10 minutes.

6 | Dampen sponge to wipe off more excess grout. Rinse the sponge and repeat until just a haze of grout remains. When the grout is completely dry, wipe off the haze with a soft flannel cloth or paper towel to shine up the glass and tile pieces.

7 | Use small paintbrush to paint the sides of each piece with glossy white paint; let dry.

8 | To finish, cut and glue felt pieces to cover the bottom of each piece. Glue rubber nonskid feet to the bottom of each trivet.

Daisy Bouquet Welcome

Hearts are a universal symbol of love, making this a perfect thing to hang on the newlyweds' front door. Cheerful daisies painted on the wooden sign wish a sunny welcome to all guests.

List of Materials

- 3/4" (2 cm) pine wood, 14" x 16" (35.5 x 40.5 cm)
- Wood filler and wood sealer
- Acrylic paints: mulberry; rose cloud; rose mist; white; light sage; crocus yellow; sandstone; pine green; forest green; burnt sienna; Payne's grey; 14K gold metallic

- Paintbrushes: Nos. 6 and 3/4" (2 cm) flat; 1/2" (1.3 cm) angular; No. 6 filbert; No. 2 round; No. 10/0 liner
- Petifour sponge
- Matte exterior varnish
- 1/8" (3 mm) gold eye hooks, four
- Gold link chain, 3" (7.5 cm)

- Pattern Sheet
- Miscellaneous items: scroll saw, palette knife, sandpaper, tack cloth, tracing paper, graphite and white transfer paper, pencil, stylus, disposable palette, water basin, paper towels, needlenose pliers

1 Refer to the Painting Instructions and Techniques on page 156. Trace the patterns; use the graphite paper and stylus to transfer the outlines to the wood. Cut out; fill any holes with wood filler. When dry, sand all surfaces smooth. Wipe with the tack cloth. Apply a coat of sealer and let it dry. Sand again lightly and wipe with the tack cloth.

2 Basecoat the heart and banner with mulberry. Let dry between paint colors, coats and each step unless otherwise indicated. Apply a second coat of mulberry. Use the white transfer paper to lightly transfer the designs, omitting the leaf veins and daisy petal detail lines.

3 Refer to the photo for placement of paints. Using rose cloud, basecoat the ribbon with the No. 6 flat brush and the banner lettering with the No. 2 round brush. Use the filbert brush to basecoat the leaves with forest green and the daisy petals with light sage. Paint flower centers with crocus yellow.

4 Use rose mist and the angular brush to shade the inside of the bow loops and the streamer curves. Shade the base of each leaf with pine green. Add a small patch of mulberry at the edge of 4 or 5 random leaves.

5 Thin sandstone to make a translucent wash. Apply a light coat to the leaves, moving the brush around on the surface to produce light and dark areas. See the Step 5 illustration to reapply the wash to 1 side of most leaves and both sides of a few leaves.

6 Use white to highlight the tip of each daisy petal and the sides of the petals in the foreground. Use burnt sienna to shade each daisy center halfway around the outer edge.

7 Highlight the folds in the bow loops and the streamer ends with white. Stroke crosswise on the ribbon using a patting motion; then quickly turn the piece and stroke the opposite side of the same area, blending with the previous stroke. Highlight the center and left edge of the bow knot.

8 Using the No. 10/0 liner and white, refer to the pattern to paint the daisy petal detail lines. Pull the lines from the flower center, varying the lengths and following the contour of the petal. Add a few light strokes of rose cloud on random petals.

9 Mix sandstone and pine green to make a very pale green. Thin the mix with water to an ink-like consistency. Then use the liner to paint the leaf veins and tendrils and to lightly outline the leaves. Use the liner and white to paint dots around the ribbon edges. Paint 2 or 3 white dots on random leaves. Use grey to paint tiny dots around the daisy centers.

10 Use the sponge to paint the sides of the heart and banner with 14K gold, including a 1/8" (3 mm) border around the front edges. Apply a second coat if needed. Apply 3 coats of varnish allowing several hours between coats. Attach the eye hooks as indicated on the patterns. Using the pliers, attach a 1½" (3.8 cm) length of chain between hooks to connect the pieces.

Wedding Ring Pillowcases

The Double Wedding Ring is one of the most beloved traditional quilting patterns. Each arc represents the unique qualities that an individual person brings to the marriage partnership. The white square between the arcs represents unity.

A variation on that pattern, this design joins the arcs in a border pattern to perk up plain white pillowcases. Paired with a quilt or a solid color comforter, they convey your best wishes for a love-filled marriage.

List of Materials

- 34" x 42" (86.5 x 107 cm) pillowcases, 1 pair
- 45" (115 cm) cotton fabrics: white solid, 1/8 yd. (0.15 m); six different green prints; six different blue prints, 6" (15 cm) square each

- Sewing threads: white polyester/cotton; clear monofilament
- 1/4" (6 mm) fusible adhesive
- Pattern Pages 164-165

- Miscellaneous items: template plastic, pencil, black fine-line permanent marker, scissors, steam iron, press cloth, sewing machine, straight pins, sewing needle

1 Wash and dry the pillowcases and fabrics without using fabric softener; press. Use the permanent marker to trace and label the patterns on template plastic. Cut out; seam allowances are included. Unless otherwise indicated, sew all fabrics right sides together using a 1/4" (6 mm) seam allowance.

2 To cut the fabric pieces, use the pencil to lightly trace the template on the wrong side of the fabric. Choose 2 blue and 2 green fabrics, then use template B to cut 4 from each fabric. Use template A to cut 4 from each of the remaining print fabrics. From the white fabric, use template C to cut 6 pieces and template D to cut 4 pieces. Mark the dots as indicated on the templates.

3 To piece each arc, use white sewing thread to sew 1 piece of each blue fabric (B, A, A, A, A, B) together along the 2³/8" (6.2 cm) sides as seen in the Step 3 illustration. Press seams to 1 side. Repeat for second arc, then reverse color order for last 2 arcs. Repeat with green fabrics.

4 Pin 1 green arc on the top of a white D, matching the center mark on D with the center seam on the inside curve of the arc. Match the end dots on D to the raw edges of the ends of the arc. Sew; remove pins. Repeat to pin and sew 1 blue arc to the opposite side of D; see the Step 3 illustration. Repeat for the remaining 3 sets.

5 To add the center square C, pin C to the end of 1 arc with the dot at the inside corner. Stitch from the outer edge to the dot; stop and clip threads. *Do not pivot.* Pin adjacent side of C to the other arc; sew. Press, then repeat to join the next arc section. Repeat to sew a center square between remaining arc sections.

6 To add the end squares, repeat Step 5 to pin and sew a C square to each end, as shown in the Step 3 illustration.

7 Follow the manufacturer's instructions to fuse 1/4" (6 mm) fusible adhesive around the curved raw edges of the pieced designs. Remove the paper backing, then turn under 1/4" (6 mm) and fuse.

8 Center and pin each pieced arc to the pillowcase hem. With monofilament in the needle and white thread in the bobbin, topstitch close to the folded edges. Pull the thread ends to the wrong side of the pillowcase and knot together. Thread ends through the embroidery needle and weave under the stitching without catching the fabric. Trim threads. Cover with press cloth and press with iron set on synthetic, avoiding direct contact between iron and monofilament.

Have a Heart Wall Quilt

Strip-piecing and rotary cutting quickly makes dozens of colorful hearts. Combine them in a pleasing pattern to create a wonderful wall quilt the bride and groom will display for years to come. To make this into a memory quilt, use a permanent marking pen to have the wedding guests sign their names on the cream strips between the rows of hearts.

List of Materials

- 45" (115 cm) cotton print fabrics: cream tone-on-tone; your choice for backing, 1 1/2 yd. (1.4 m) each; dark red for border; green for binding, 1/2 yd. (0.5 m) each; medium blue; green; tan; three assorted reds, 1/2 yd. (0.5 m) each for the hearts
- Low-loft cotton quilt batting, 45" x 60" (115 x 152.5 cm)

- Threads: matching sewing; cream quilting
- Needles: sewing; quilting
- Miscellaneous items: iron, scissors, rotary cutter, mat and clear ruler with 45° angle markings, tape measure, sewing machine, straight pins

1. Wash and dry all fabrics; press. Sew all fabrics right sides together using a 1/4" (6 mm) seam allowance. Press the seams open unless otherwise indicated. Rotary cut the following fabric strips: 3 1/4" x 45" (8.2 x 115 cm) border print, 4; 2" x 45" (5 x 115 cm) green binding print, 4; 2" x 45" (5 x 115 cm) cream tone-on-tone print, 24; and 3" x 45" (7.5 x 115 cm) medium blue, green, tan and 3 assorted dark red prints, 2 each.

2″

2 1/2″

2 1/2″

Rotary cut 11 strips from each 3-strip group at a 45° angle that are 2 1/2″ wide

2. To piece the heart blocks, see the Step 2 illustration to sew 1 of each color heart fabric strip between 2 cream fabric strips, staggering the strips 2" (5 cm). With the second strip of each color, repeat to sew strips staggered in the opposite direction. Use the rotary cutter, ruler and mat to cut each strip at a 45° angle every 2 1/2" (6.5 cm) for a total of 11 angled strips. As shown, angle the ruler the same direction as the staggered ends.

3. Align the seams and sew 2 strips of the same color, but opposite angles, together. See the Step 3 illustration. To cut the blocks, align each pieced section along a straight line of the cutting mat. Trim off the bottom of the section 1/4" (6 mm) below the bottom point of the colored print as shown; discard. Cut 4 1/2" (11.5 cm) above the first cut to make a 4 1/2" (11.5 cm) square block. Cut 1 5/8" (4 cm) above the second cut to make a 1 5/8" x 4 1/2" (4 x 11.5 cm) strip. Discard the remaining points.

4. Alternating the red heart blocks with the other colors, arrange 8 blocks in a horizontal row. Make 3 different horizontal rows (A, B, C); sew each row of blocks together. Repeat to make 8 rows total as follows: 3 A; 3 B; 3 C. Repeat to sew the 1 5/8" x 4 1/2" (4 x 11.5 cm) strips in 8 horizontal rows.

5. Align the seams and sew a row of strips to the top edge of each row of hearts. Sew alternating A, B and C rows together to assemble the quilt center. Sew a 3 1/4" (8.2 cm) border strip to both sides of the quilt center; trim the ends even. Press the seams toward the border fabric. Repeat to sew the remaining borders to the top and bottom of the quilt center.

Third cut

Second cut

First cut

Discard

1 5/8″

4 1/2″

Discard

1/4″

Stitch strips together here

6. Layer the quilt backing wrong side up, the batting, and the quilt top right side up. Baste the layers together from the center to the edges in vertical and horizontal rows. Baste around the quilt top close to the edges. Trim any excess batting and backing fabric. Beginning at the center and working outward, hand quilt 1/4" (6 mm) inside every other heart or each heart, if desired. Remove all basting stitches except around the edges.

7. To bind the quilt, sew the 2" (5 cm) strips together to make 1 long strip. Fold it in half lengthwise, wrong sides together, and press. Turn under 1 raw end 1/4" (6 mm), align the raw edges and sew the binding around the quilt top, overlapping the ends and mitering the corners. Turn the binding to the back of the quilt and slipstitch in place.

Topiary Fantasy

This combination of ivy, grapevines and moss will make a splendid addition to the happy couple's home. Made of silks and drieds, it will stay beautiful with no watering, pruning or training needed, just a light dusting every once in a while. Geometric shapes like this are very popular now, and you can make it yourself at a fraction of what it would cost purchased in an exclusive boutique.

Assembly Guide

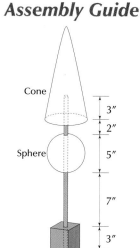

Cone

3″

2″

Sphere 5″

7″

3″

Brick

List of Materials

- Acrylic craft paints: metallic gold, burgundy, teal
- 20″ (51 cm) wooden dowel, 3/8″ (1 cm) thick
- 3″ x 4″ x 8″ (7.5 x 10 x 20.5 cm) floral foam brick
- Styrofoam®: 4″ x 12″ (10 x 30.5 cm) cone, 5″ (12.5 cm) ball
- 40″ (102 cm) of 22-gauge craft wire
- 24 oz. (750 mL) papier-mâché mix
- Plastic canvas circle or plastic doily for texture (optional)
- 8″ (20.5 cm) terra cotta pot
- 12 twigs, 7″ (18 cm) long

- Moss: 1 bag each Spanish and reindeer
- 9 ft. (274.5 cm) silk ivy
- Floral pins
- 12″ (30.5 cm) grapevine wreath
- 3 yd. (2.75 m) gold mesh craft ribbon, 1 1/2″ (3.8 cm) wide
- Miscellaneous items: sponge paintbrush, paint palette, measuring tape, pencil, hammer, nail, craft glue, scissors, paper towels, newspaper, mixing bowl, measuring cup, small sponge, electric fan (optional), cooling rack, soft rag or natural sponge, serrated knife, hot glue gun, plastic lid, several cups of rocks

1. Let all paints dry between colors and coats. Use sponge brush to paint dowel metallic gold. Refer to the photo and the Assembly Guide throughout to make and assemble the topiary. Measure and mark the foam pieces for the dowel as follows: center of 1 short end of the brick, the bottom circle of the cone, and the center on 2 opposite sides of the sphere.

2. Poke a nail through each side of the sphere to start a path, force the dowel through, then remove. Use the hammer to gently tap the dowel 3″ (7.5 cm) into the marked spot on the brick and cone. Remove the dowel, and pour craft glue into the brick hole and along the dowel. Force dowel back into the brick, and let dry for 1 hour.

3. Lay the brick and dowel flat on a work surface. Measure and mark the dowel 7″ (18 cm) and 12″ (30.5 cm) above the brick. Coat the dowel with glue between those marks, and pour glue into the sphere hole. Slide the sphere onto the dowel, and let dry for 1 hour; wipe excess glue off. Cut two 12″ (30.5 cm) pieces of wire. Fold each piece in half, and wrap tightly around the dowel on each side of the sphere to prevent slippage; tuck ends into the foam.

4. Cover work surface with newspaper. Mix papier-mâché according to directions, about 5 cups (1.2 L) of water for 24 oz. (710 mL); let the mixture stand for 15 minutes. Lay brick/dowel/sphere structure flat, and apply small amounts of pulp to the sphere. Use the sponge to press pulp onto foam and remove excess water. Cover entire surface 1/4″ to 1/2″ (6 mm to 1.3 cm) thick; if desired, texture the surface with plastic canvas or doily. Repeat to cover the cone from top to bottom, placing it upright on the work surface. Stand the dowel structure upright in the clay pot (stuff with rags or newspaper to hold), and the cone on a cooling rack. Let dry 1-2 days in front of a fan, rotating every 2 hours to dry evenly, or 1 day in full sunshine.

5. Use rag to apply burgundy paint, thinned with water, liberally to the sphere and cone. Work paint into any textured areas, and coat completely. Lightly sponge teal, then gold. Wipe the clay pot with the burgundy paint to lightly coat the pot. Use a damp rag to wipe back over, creating a stained effect.

6. Cut remaining wire into two 8″ (20.5 cm) pieces. Take 6 twigs and insert them into the brick, making a fence around the dowel. Wrap the loose upper ends of the twigs with wire, and tuck ends into bottom of the sphere. Repeat with the remaining twigs, inserting the ends into the bottom of the sphere, and wiring down by the brick.

7. Place the brick in the pot; trim the bottom with a serrated knife until the brick top sits even with the bottom of the rim and the brick bottom rests on the pot bottom. Coat the brick sides and bottom with glue where it has contact with the pot, and vice versa. Force and secure the brick into the pot. Place a plastic lid or paper plate under the pot to catch excess glue. Place rocks into the pot around the brick for stability. Pour glue in between the rocks as you go to hold them in place until they are flush with the brick.

8. Hot-glue 3 spiral lines around the sphere. Working on 1 line at a time, from top to bottom, hot-glue liberally along the lines, and apply reindeer moss. Vary the thickness of the moss for interest. Repeat to apply a continuous thin spiral around the cone, making about 5 loops. Pour craft glue into the cone hole and along the dowel, and place cone on the dowel.

9. Cut ivy into the following lengths: two 18″ (46 cm), 24″ (61 cm) and 36″ (91.5 cm). Take 1 end of an 18″ (46 cm) piece and dip it in glue. Insert into the brick, then wind the ivy up around the dowels/twigs and glue the other end into the sphere bottom. Repeat with the other short piece, beginning and ending on opposite sides of the brick and sphere. Glue 1 end of the 36″ (91.5 cm) piece into the cone bottom, and loosely wind it around the cone following the reindeer moss; glue the end into the cone top. Cut the remaining ivy into 4 pieces. Place them vertically on the sphere dividing it into quarters; glue ends into the sphere top and bottom. Anchor the ivy where desired using floral pins dipped in glue and inserted into the foam.

10. Apply hot glue to the rock tops; cover with Spanish moss. Undo the grapevine wreath and separate out two 40″ (102 cm) pieces. Dip 1 end in glue and insert into the brick, wind to the top, and insert in the cone. Repeat with the other piece, beginning and ending on opposite sides of the brick and sphere. Use floral pins to hold the ribbon in place at top and bottom, and weave it in and out of the grapevine, spiraling in the opposite direction.

Babies

New parents need a lot of things for the new addition to the family! While you can't give them a good night's sleep, you can create a one-of-a-kind baby gift. From the pretty, to the practical, to the just plain fun, your gift for the baby will be the hit of the shower!

naptime Afghan

Nine baby granny squares and double crochet stitches make an exquisitely soft afghan to cover the little one. You'll be surprised how fast it takes shape. With only four easy stitches, this is a perfect project for beginners to take on. Worked in baby blue and white for a boy, or pink and white for a girl, it will be a hit at the shower.

List of Materials

- Baby pompadour sportweight yarn, 6-oz. (170 g) skeins: white (A), one; blue (B), three
- Size G crochet hook
- Yarn needle
- Scissors

1 See the Crochet Abbreviations and Stitches on page 161. Ch 3 at beginning of round counts as double crochet.
Finished Afghan Size: 37" (94 cm) square

2 To crochet a square, with color A, ch 5, join with sl st to form ring.
Rnd 1: Ch 3, 2 dc in ring (ch 2, 3 dc in ring), 3 times, ch 2, (sl st in top of beg ch-3, next 2 dc and sp); four corners made.
Rnd 2: Ch 3, 2 dc in sp, ch 2, 3 dc in same sp, ch 1, in corner work (3 dc, ch 2, 3 dc) 3 times, ch 1, (sl st in top of beg ch-3, next 2 dc and sp). Fasten off.
Rnd 3: Attach color B in corner. Ch 3, 2 dc in sp, ch 2, 3 dc in same sp, ch 1, 3 dc in next sp, ch 1; in next corner work (3 dc, ch 2, 3 dc) 3 times, ch 1, 3 dc in next sp, ch 1, (sl st in top of beg ch-3, next 2 dc and sp). Fasten off.
Rnd 4: Attach color A in corner. Ch 3, 2 dc in sp, ch 2, 3 dc in same sp, *ch 1, (in each ch-1 sp, work 3 dc, ch 1) across side. In next corner, work 3 dc, ch 2, 3 dc. Repeat from * 3 times ending last repeat with (sl st in top of beg ch-3, next 2 dc and sp). Fasten off.
Rnd 5: Attach color B in corner. Ch 3, 2 dc in sp, ch 2, 3 dc in same sp, *ch 1, (in each ch-1 sp make 3 dc, ch 1) across side, in next corner work 3 dc, ch 2, 3 dc. Repeat from * 3 times ending last repeat with (sl st in top of beg ch-3, next 2 dc and sp).
Rnd 6: Repeat Rnd 5. Fasten off.

3 Repeat to crochet 9 squares and stitch together with color B.

4 Attach color A in corner.
Rnd 7: Ch 3, 2 dc in sp, ch 2, 3 dc in same sp, *ch 1, (in each sp make 3 dc, ch 1) across side; in next corner make 3 dc, ch 2, 3 dc. Repeat from * 3 times except instead of final corner, (sl st in top of beg ch-3, next 2 dc and sp). (20 ch-1 sp per side).
Rnds 8-9: Continue with color A; repeat Rnd 5. Fasten off.
Rnd 10: Attach color B; repeat Rnd 5; fasten off.
Rnd 11: Attach color A; repeat Rnd 5; fasten off.
Rnds 12-16: Attach color B; repeat Rnd 5; fasten off.
Rnd 17: Attach color A; repeat Rnd 5; fasten off.
Rnds 18-22: Attach color B; repeat Rnd 5; fasten off.
Rnd 23: Attach color A; repeat Rnd 5; fasten off.
Rnds 24-28: Attach color B; repeat Rnd 5; fasten off.
Rnd 29: Attach color A; repeat Rnd 5; fasten off.
Rnds 30-31: Attach color B; repeat Rnd 5; fasten off.

5 **Rnd 32:** For the edging, sc in corner sp, *(ch 3, 2 dc and sc in corner sp) 2 times; (ch 3, 2 dc in same sp, sc in next sp) across side. Repeat from * 3 times except instead of final sc, sl st in 1st sc; fasten off.

Ribbon Embroidered Baby Outfit

Delicate ribbon embroidery changes store-bought togs into an adorable embellished baby outfit for your precious little one.

List of Materials

- White baby dress with yoke
- Matching fabric baby booties
- 4 mm embroidery ribbon: light pink; blue; willow green
- Silk embroidery thread: green; gold
- Embroidery floss, pink
- Glass seed beads, pearl
- Needles: No. 24 crewel; beading
- Miscellaneous items: tracing paper, pencil, white sewing thread

1 Refer to the Ribbon Embroidery Stitches on page 159 to stitch the design.

2 To embroider the dress, trace the Ribbon Embroidery Guide. Slip Guide under dress yoke and center. Lightly pencil center of spider web rose, daisies and ends of curved stems.

3 To make the spider web rose, use 2 strands of pink floss to stitch the spokes for the base and pink ribbon to work the rose.

4 To make each daisy, use blue ribbon to work 5 lazy daisy stitches around the center. Use 2 strands of gold silk thread to work 4 single wrap French knots in the daisy center.

5 Use 2 strands of green silk thread to work the stems in stem stitch and to work lazy daisy leaves around the daisies.

6 Use green ribbon to work 3 lazy daisy leaves on each side of rose with center leaf slightly longer.

7 Use white sewing thread to attach beads at stem ends.

8 To embroider each bootie, refer to the photo and see Step 3 to center 1 pink spider web rose on toe of bootie. See Step 6 to stitch 3 leaves on each side of rose.

Ribbon Embroidery Guide

Ribbon Embroidered Baby Outfit Color/Stitch Key

Stitch	Color
⊗ Spider Web Rose	Pink Floss & Ribbon
⟋ Lazy Daisy Stitch	Blue Ribbon
⟋ Lazy Daisy Stitch	Green Silk Thread
⟋ Lazy Daisy Stitch	Green Ribbon
⟋ Stem Stitch	Green Silk Thread
• French Knots	Gold Silk Thread
• Pearl Seed Bead	

Baby Bathtime

Nine months of anticipation and baby is finally here! Celebrate the happy occasion with beautiful handmade gifts. Two color variations let you work the hooded towel, burp cloth and bath mitt in pink or blue!

List of Materials

- White cotton terry hooded baby towel with 14-count evenweave insert*
- White cotton terry baby accessories with 14-count Aida band*; burp cloth; bath mitt
- 6-strand Anchor embroidery floss in colors listed in the Color Key

- No. 24 tapestry needle
- Pattern Page 170
- Miscellaneous items: scissors, ruler
- *(See Sources on pg. 175 for purchasing information.)

1 Refer to the Cross-Stitch General Instructions and Stitches on page 160 and the Stitch Charts here and on page 170 to work the designs. Use the appropriate Color Key for pink baby girl or blue baby boy items. Begin stitching where indicated for each item, starting at the top of the chart. Work the cross-stitches using 2 strands of floss and the backstitches with 1 strand.

2 To stitch the hooded towel, measure 2³/₄" (7 cm) from the top corner of the evenweave insert to begin stitching.

3 To stitch the burp cloth, find the center of the short bound edge of the band and count down 4 rows to begin stitching.

4 To stitch the bath mitt, find the center of the gingham binding and count down 3 rows on the band to begin stitching.

Burp Cloth/Bath Mitt
Stitch Chart 1 of 2
(Hooded Towel Stitch Chart is on page 170)

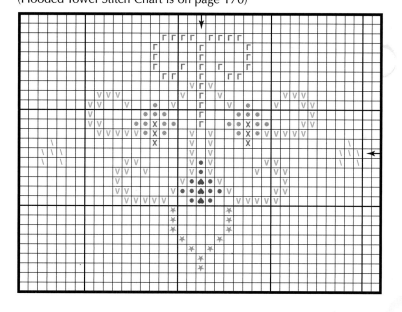

Baby Girl Color Key

Symbol	Anchor #	Color
♥	76	Med. Antique Rose
/	77	Med. Dk. Antique Rose
X	144	Vy. Lt. Delft Blue
•	145	Lt. Delft Blue
∧	203	Lt. Mint Green
L	204	Med. Mint Green
★	206	Lt. Spruce
•	300	Lt. Citrus

Baby Boy Color Key

Symbol	Anchor #	Color
X	25	Lt. Carnation
•	76	Med. Antique Rose
♥	145	Lt. Delft Blue
∧	203	Lt. Mint Green
L	204	Med. Mint Green
★	206	Lt. Spruce
•	300	Lt. Citrus
/	977	Med. Sea Blue

Rainbow of Bunnies Bib

Bunny rabbits in the colors of the rainbow will brighten baby's outfit and bring a smile to everyone who sees it. This simple design will stitch up quickly, so you may want to make more than one bib. As everyone knows, one little baby can make a very big mess!

List of Materials

- Prefinished bib with a 4" x 8¾" (10 x 22.4 cm) 14-count Aida fabric insert
- 6-strand skeins of DMC embroidery floss in colors listed in Color Key
- No. 24 tapestry needle
- Miscellaneous items: scissors, iron, terrycloth towel

1. Refer to Cross-Stitch Instructions and Stitches on page 160. Symbols correspond to colors in the Color Key. Each square on the chart represents 1 square of Aida.

2. Refer to the Stitch Chart to stitch the design. Work cross-stitches with 3 strands of floss. Use 2 strands to work the following backstitches and French knots: peach bunny, dark terra cotta (355); green bunny, Christmas green (699); yellow bunny, very dark topaz (781); lavender bunny, very dark violet (550). Backstitch balloon strings with only 1 strand of floss.

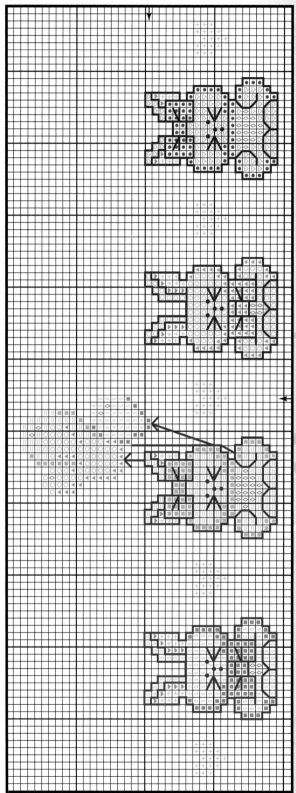

Rainbow of Bunnies Bib
Color Key

Symbol	DMC #	Color
		White
◇	209	Dk. Lavender
●	211	Lt. Lavender
▷	352	Lt. Coral
◀	353	Peach
○	727	Vy. Lt. Topaz
‖	743	Med. Yellow
▦	913	Med. Nile Green
▧	955	Lt. Nile Green
⦰	962	Medium Dusty Rose
▶	3716	Vy. Lt. Dusty Rose
+		Backstitches
❙ ●		French Knots

Terrycloth Teddy Bear

From his blanket stitched paws to plaid bow tie and blushing cheeks, this li'l 10" (25.5 cm) bear is as lovable as can be. Cut his face and inner body from wood and his "fur" from a brown terrycloth hand towel. Don't tell anyone, but Teddy has been snacking—he's stuffed with popcorn, making his beanbag body oh so cuddly!

List of Materials

- 3/4" (2 cm) pine wood, 4" x 6" (10 x 15 cm)
- Brown terrycloth hand towel
- Cotton print fabric, 1 3/4" x 16" (4.5 x 40.5 cm)
- Tan felt, 2" (5 cm) square
- Black embroidery floss

- Needles: sewing; embroidery
- Acrylic paints: light brown; red; black; white
- Paintbrushes: fine liner; small stencil; 1" (2.5 cm) foam
- Unpopped popcorn kernels for stuffing, 1 cup (250 mL)
- Glues: wood; hot glue gun

- Scroll saw
- Pattern Sheet
- Miscellaneous items: pencil, scissors, tracing and graphite paper, fine sandpaper, tack cloth, stylus, ruler, measuring cup, sewing machine, matching sewing threads

1 Refer to the Painting Instructions and Techniques on page 156. Trace the patterns to tracing paper. Use graphite paper and stylus to transfer face/inner body and muzzle onto wood; cut out. Sand to smooth rough edges and wipe with tack cloth.

2 Basecoat front of face brown extending color onto edges; let dry. Use wood glue to glue unpainted muzzle lengthwise to face. Refer to the photo and pattern to paint a black nose on front tip, then mouth lines. Also paint black eyes and eyelashes on each side of muzzle top. Dot eyes with white highlights. Use stencil brush to stipple red paint on cheeks.

3 Cut out fabrics as indicated. Refer to the Embroidery Stitches on page 159 to blanket stitch paws with black floss to bottom of arms on body front.

4 To sew the bear, sew fabrics using a 1/4" (6 mm) seam allowance. Sew body front pieces together along center seam, ending at dot. Repeat to sew back pieces. Sew front of back, leaving top open; turn.

5 Lightly stuff feet/legs with popcorn. Refer to the pattern stitching line to hand stitch across top of each leg to keep popcorn in place. Repeat to stuff each arm, stitching from shoulder to underarm.

6 Insert wood body inside cloth body, then add popcorn in front and back of wood to lightly stuff, as shown in the Step 6 illustration. Turn under and sew gathering stitches around top body edge; gather tightly and knot thread.

7 Turn under and sew straight edge of head back. Sew head top around curved edge of head back, then place on wood head. Turn under front edge near face and glue to wood sides. Also glue bottom back of head to wood.

8 Pair and sew ears together leaving straight edge open; turn. Refer to the photo to fold ears in half and glue to top of head. Tie fabric strip in bow around neck.

Duck Pull Toy

For generations, young children have enjoyed walking around with a string in hand, pulling a toy behind them. Reminiscent of the wood toys of yesteryear, this wood cutout mother duck and her ducklings sit happily on wood bases with wheels. A string with a bead on the end makes it easy for little hands to pull, and the connectors between the pieces can be easily removed for play.

List of Materials

- Pine wood: 1/2" (1.3 cm), 8" x 10" (20.5 x 25.5 cm); 1" (2.5 cm), 6" x 8" (15 x 20.5 cm)
- Wood dowels: 3/16" (4.5 mm), three 1/2" (1.3 cm) pieces; 1/4" (6 mm), four 2" (5 cm) pieces
- Wood wheels: 1 1/2" (3.8 cm) with pegs, four; 1" (2.5 cm), eight
- Acrylic paints: black, yellow, orange, tapioca, slate blue

- Paintbrushes: No. 6 flat; 10/0 liner; 1" (2.5 cm) sponge
- Waterbase satin varnish
- Orange satin ribbon, 3/8" (1 cm), 1 yd. (0.95 m)
- White nylon cord, 2/3 yd. (0.63 m)
- Wood craft sticks, two
- 20 mm wood bead

- Thick craft glue
- Scroll saw
- Drill with 3/16", 5/16" 1/4", 7/64", and 13/64" bits
- Pattern Page 167
- Miscellaneous items: tracing paper, transfer paper, disposable palette, scissors, fine sandpaper, ruler, pencil

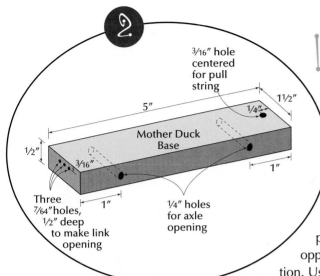

2

3/16″ hole centered for pull string

5″

1½″

¼″

Mother Duck Base

½″

3/16″

1″

1″

Three 7/64″ holes, ½″ deep to make link opening

¼″ holes for axle opening

Refer to the Painting Instructions and Techniques on page 156. Trace the patterns onto tracing paper. Transfer to wood pieces indicated on patterns and cut out. Also, from ½″ (1.3 cm) wood, cut one 1½″ x 5″ (3.8 x 12.5 cm) piece for the mother duck base and two 1⅛″ x 2¼″ (2.8 x 6 cm) pieces for the duckling bases. Drill holes on craft stick links as indicated. Sand edges.

2 For the mother duck base, measure 1″ (2.5 cm) from each end on long sides and mark with a pencil. Use the ¼″ bit to drill through side of base to opposite side for axle openings; refer to the Step 2 illustration. Use the 7/64″ bit to drill 3 closely spaced holes ½″ (1.3 cm) deep on 1 short end. Move bit back and forth between holes to remove wood and make an opening for the link. Glue flat end of link into opening. On opposite short end, center and drill a 3/16″ (4.5 mm) hole through base from top to bottom, ¼″ (6 mm) from edge.

3 For each duckling base, measure ½″ (1.3 cm) from each end on long sides and mark with a pencil. Use the 5/16″ bit to drill through side of the base to opposite side for axle openings. To add the link posts to the base tops, pencil a centered mark 3/16″ (4.5 mm) from each end on 1 base, and 1 end on remaining base. Use the 3/16″ bit to drill ¼″ (6 mm) deep holes at marks.

4 Use slate blue to paint the bases, 3/16″ (4.5 mm) dowel pieces, links and the wood bead. Basecoat the mother duck with tapioca paint and the ducklings with yellow on the backs, sides and fronts. Paint beaks with orange. Let dry. Outline beaks and mother duck wings with black; dot the eyes. Let dry.

5 Apply 2 coats of varnish to all pieces, letting dry between coats.

6 To finish the mother duck base, glue wheel pegs into holes, cutting pegs shorter if necessary. Insert 1 end of nylon cord through hole in base, and knot securely on bottom. String bead on opposite end of cord; tie a knot on each side of bead to secure. Glue mother duck to center top of base.

¼″ deep holes for 3/16″ dowel link posts

2¼″

3/16″

Middle Duckling Base

½″

1⅛″

½″

¼″ dowel axles through 5/16″ holes

7

7 To finish each duckling base, see the Step 7 illustration to insert ¼″ (6 mm) dowels through axle holes and glue wheels to dowel ends. Glue 3/16″ (4.5 mm) dowels into holes on top of each base for link posts. Glue duckling to top of each base, allowing room for links to slide easily onto posts.

8 Cut a 15″ (38 cm) piece of ribbon in half and tie each into a bow. Glue to front side of each duckling's neck. Attach ducks by sliding links over posts. Glue remaining ribbon around mother duck's neck, and tie into a bow.

Baby Express

Show your love for the little one with this charming choo-choo specially made to hold baby necessities. Simply say, "I think I can, I think I can," and in no time you'll have this mini 10" (25.5 cm) train assembled. Button wheels and a puff of batting "smoke" add the finishing touches.

List of Materials

- 14-count white perforated plastic, one sheet
- 6-skein Anchor embroidery floss in colors listed in Color Key
- No. 24 tapestry needle
- 7/8" (2.2 cm) white two-hole flat buttons, 12
- Pattern Pages 168-169
- Miscellaneous items: small pointed scissors, ruler, indelible marker, masking tape, cotton ball

1 Refer to the Perforated Plastic Instructions and Stitches on page 160. Cut the following pieces from perforated plastic:

For Engine:	one 21x22-squares for front
	two 33x43-squares for sides
	two 33x22-squares for cab front and back
	one 22x40-squares for bottom
	one 20x27-squares for smoke stack
For Boxcar:	two 21x42-squares for sides
	two 21x22-squares for front and back
	one 22x42-squares for bottom
For Caboose:	two 33x43-squares for sides
	two 22x33-squares for front and back
	one 22x37-squares for bottom

2 Trim the following pieces according to bold outlines on the Stitch Charts on pages 168-169: engine sides, front, smokestack and cab front; boxcar sides and caboose sides. Do not cut out windows until stitching is complete. Use masking tape and marker to label each piece.

3 Find the design center by following the arrows on the Stitch Charts. Count up and over to the top left corner of the design to begin stitching. Cross-stitch using 3 strands of floss and overcast using 6 strands. Symbols correspond to colors in the Color Key.

4 To assemble the engine, cut out windows. Use white floss to overcast sides, front, and back to the bottom panel. To tack on the button wheels, see the Stitch Chart for placement, using white floss.

5 Cut slits with craft knife at engine sides as shown on Stitch Charts. Overcast the engine sides together along the top on either side of the smokestack. Overcast the engine front to the engine side. Insert cab front behind the engine front, then overcast cab sides together.

6 Roll the smokestack into a cylinder, overlapping 3 blank squares, then overcast. Wedge the smokestack into the engine hole. Use a small piece of cotton in smokestack to simulate smoke.

7 To assemble the boxcar and caboose, refer to Step 4 to assemble and tack on the wheels. Overcast sides together.

8 To connect each car 3/4" (2 cm) apart, count 4 squares up and over from each bottom corner. Knot end of 6 strands of white floss and thread through the first car into the second car; knot end of the floss inside car.

shhh... Baby's Asleep

Use a quick and easy salt dough recipe to create this darling bear door hanger. Hanging from colorful satin ribbon, this balsa wood sign warns all passersby not to wake the baby. This delightful bear is a great gift for an older child too; simply personalize the sign with the child's name.

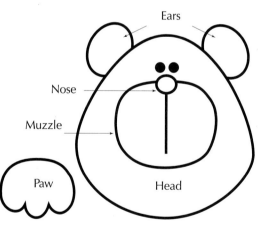

Ears

Nose

Muzzle

Paw

Head

List of Materials

- Salt dough ingredients: 4 cups (1 L) flour; 1¹/₂ cups (375 mL) salt; 1 cup (250 mL) sugar; ¹/₄ cup (50 mL) glycerin; 1¹/₂ cups (375 mL) water
- Acrylic paints: white; black; antique white; pink; tan
- Paintbrushes: fine liner; small flat

- ¹/₄" x 2¹/₄" x 4" (6 mm x 6 cm x 10 cm) balsa wood
- ¹/₄" (6 mm) double-face satin ribbon, your choice, 1 yd. (0.95 m)
- Black permanent marking pens: fine point; extra fine point
- Hot glue gun

- Miscellaneous items: nonstick saucepan, large glass bowl, plastic bag, mixing spoon, tracing paper, pencil, craft knife, scissors, metal edge ruler, cutting surface, small sharp knife, round toothpick, disposable palette, container for water, nonstick cookie sheet, cookie rack, oven

1 Place the water, salt, sugar and glycerin in a saucepan and bring to a boil. Reduce heat to medium and continue to cook for 5 minutes. Set the mix aside to cool for 10 minutes, then add it to the flour in a large glass bowl and stir until the mixture holds together.

2 When the dough is cool enough to handle, turn it out onto the counter and knead it for several minutes until it is smooth and elastic. If it's too dry, add a small amount of water; if it's too moist, add flour. Salt dough should be fairly stiff so it will hold its shape, but should not be too dry.

3 Store the dough in a plastic bag and refrigerate it until ready to use. Dough can be kept for 3 days. If it becomes sticky, add small amounts of flour to bring it back to the correct consistency.

4 To make the bear, trace the patterns onto tracing paper. Roll the following dough pieces, referring to the pattern for size and shape: one 1½" (3.8 cm) ball head; two ½" (1.3 cm) ball ears; one 3/16" (4.5 mm) ball nose; two ½" (1.3 cm) ball paws; and one ½" (1.3 cm) ball muzzle. Flatten the muzzle ball and attach it to the bear's head/face. To join dough pieces, use a liner brush and a small amount of water to adhere pieces before baking. Press a small knife vertically against the muzzle to create the center line.

5 Refer to the pattern and the Step 5 illustration to attach the ears and nose to the head. To make the eyes, refer to the photo to press the paintbrush handle into the dough just above the muzzle. Use a toothpick to make a hole in the center bottom of the head. Place the bear's head and each paw on a nonstick cookie sheet and bake at 225° (107°C) for about 1 hour. Place the pieces on a cookie rack to cool.

6 To make the sign, basecoat the balsa with 2 coats of antique white. Let dry between each coat and each color unless otherwise indicated. Use the fine-point pen to draw the outer squiggly border about ¼" (6 mm) from the sign edges. Use the extra-fine-point pen to draw the inner squiggly border. Using the fine-point pen, center the saying, replacing "Baby" with a name, if desired.

7 When the salt dough pieces have cooled, carefully paint the head and paws tan, the muzzle white and the nose pink. Dip the paintbrush handle in black to paint the eyes. Let dry.

8 To assemble the door hanger, push 1 end of the toothpick into the center top of the balsa sign, then gently push the bear's head onto the other end of the toothpick. Glue the bottom of the head to the top of the balsa for added support. Refer to the photo to glue the paws to the sign.

9 Cut the ribbon into three 12" (30.5 cm) lengths. Tie 1 length into a 2" (5 cm) bow and trim the streamer ends. Glue it under the bear's chin. Glue 1 end of each remaining length to the back of the sign, head and ear to hold the sign straight. Tie the ends together in a 2" (5 cm) bow. Trim streamers as needed.

Ear

Ear

Nose

Muzzle

5

Summertime Crocheted Booties

A cool and cute gift for the newborn, these adorable booties are quick to make (about two hours per pair). Choose whatever fun color of pearl cotton you'd like, and use two colors of coordinating rickrack as the inset.

List of Materials

- No. 5 pearl cotton, 25-meter skeins, two, your color choice
- Jumbo rickrack, two colors, your choice, ½ yd. (0.5 m) each
- Size 8 crochet hook or size to obtain gauge
- Miscellaneous items: scissors, matching thread, sewing needle, ruler

1   To crochet the booties, refer to the Crochet Stitches
and Abbreviations on page 161.

Size: 1-3 months.

Gauge: 9 tr = 1 inch.

2   See the Step 2 illustration to
make twisted rickrack trim.
Twist 2 lengths of rickrack around
each other so that they interlock and
form 24 points on each side. Make
a circle of the rickrack and tuck the
beginning and ending tails inside. Stitch
them in place with needle and thread.

3   Begin at the center of the sole and ch 24.

Rnd 1: Work 11 tr in 3rd ch from hook, tr in each of next 20
ch, 10 tr in last ch, tr in between each ch-tr on opposite side; join.

Rnd 2: Ch 3 (counts as first tr) sk 1st st, (2 tr in each st) 10 times, 11 tr,
dc, 28 sc, dc, 10 tr; join. (72 sts)

Rnd 3: Ch 3 (counts as first tr), (3 tr, sl st in point of trim) around; join.
Fasten off. (72 tr—96 sts) To crochet through the trim easily, wiggle the
crochet hook until it pierces the trim. Push the hook well into the trim so
that the flaring shank of the crochet hook enlarges the hole in the trim.
Yarn over and pull the thread through the hole (the hook won't catch on
the trim).

4   At the heel, determine the center back point of the trim, counting 9
points on the upper edge of the trim around the heel. Move to the
fourth point to the right of the center point, and attach thread at this point.
You will be crocheting back toward the center of the heel, then on around
to the left.

Rnd 4: (Ch 3, sl st in next point) 12 times, (ch 1, sl st in next point) 9 times,
(ch 3, sl st in next point) 2 times, ch 3; join.

Rnd 5: Ch 1, sc over each ch of previous rnd; join.

Rnd 6: Ch 1, 46 sc, ch 6, sl st in 35th sc of same rnd, sl st into 34th sc of
same rnd, 10 sc around ch 6 just made, sc in rem sts; join.

Rnd 7: Ch 35, sk 1 ch, sc in each ch st just made, 24 sc in previous rnd sc
sts, ch 35, sk 1 ch, sc in each ch st just made, sl st in 25th sc of previous
rnd. Fasten off.

Faux Finish Frame

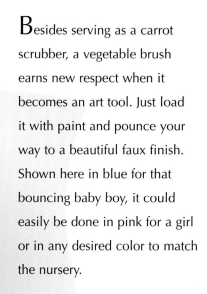

Besides serving as a carrot scrubber, a vegetable brush earns new respect when it becomes an art tool. Just load it with paint and pounce your way to a beautiful faux finish. Shown here in blue for that bouncing baby boy, it could easily be done in pink for a girl or in any desired color to match the nursery.

List of Materials

- Wood frame, your choice
- White stain blocking primer
- 1" (2.5 cm) sponge brush
- Semigloss latex or acrylic paint: white; periwinkle blue

- Vegetable brush
- Waterbase semigloss polyurethane varnish
- Clear acrylic spray

- Miscellaneous items: fine sandpaper, tack cloth, disposable palette, palette knife, paper towels, measuring cup

1 Use the 1″ (2.5 cm) brush to basecoat the surface with white stain blocking primer. Let dry between paint colors and coats, and each step. Lightly sand the surface, and wipe with a tack cloth.

2 Use the 1″ (2.5 cm) brush to basecoat the surface in white semigloss latex or acrylic paint. Apply 2 to 3 coats of the white basecoat color to achieve a nice opaque coverage.

3 Pour approximately 1/3 cup (75 mL) of periwinkle blue paint onto the center of the palette. Add approximately 1/6 cup (40 mL) of varnish. Mix thoroughly with a palette knife. The consistency should be that of "cream soup" for pouncing the color.

4 Fold 3 paper towels in quarters. Load the vegetable brush with a light amount of pouncing paint. Tap the brush onto the folded stack of paper towels to remove any excess and to evenly spread the blue paint on the vegetable brush. This will help prevent large blotchy areas of paint on the surface. Begin by lightly "hitting" or pouncing the surface of the object to create a varied stippled pattern, as shown in the Step 4 illustration.

5 As the paint fades on the vegetable brush, reload the brush with fresh color and tap on paper towels. Continue lightly pouncing the surface until a pleasing overall pattern is achieved. If any area appears to have too much of the blue pounced color, load the vegetable brush with the white basecoat color and hit the surface to "open up" that area of color.

6 Seal and protect the frame with several light mistings of clear acrylic spray, or brush on 2 coats of varnish.

Six of Hearts Frame

A new baby means lots of pictures, and this frame will be a great way for parents to show photos off or give them as gifts. Best of all, it's easy enough for anyone to craft. Adhere parchment paper to a magnetic sheet, cut out the wallet-size photo openings, and glue on fabric hearts and buttons.

List of Materials

- Adhesive-backed magnetic sheet, 8½" x 11" (21.8 x 28 cm)
- Gold parchment paper
- Mini-print cotton fabrics, 3" (7.5 cm) squares, six assorted
- Coordinating small buttons, 25-30
- Black permanent fine-line marking pen
- White craft glue
- Wallet-size photos, three
- Pattern Sheet
- Miscellaneous items: sharp pencil, tracing and wax-free transfer paper, ruler, scissors, craft knife, cutting board or rotary cutter mat, transparent tape, access to photocopy machine (optional)

1 Trace the frame pattern to tracing paper. Place the transfer paper between the tracing and the parchment paper and use a sharp pencil to transfer the pattern lines. If desired, the frame pattern may be photocopied directly onto the parchment.

2 From the magnetic sheet, cut an 8^1/$_2$" x 11" (21.8 x 28 cm) piece. Remove the paper backing (do not discard), then adhere the magnetic sheet to the wrong side of the parchment paper. To keep the parchment clean, place the paper backing on your work surface, then the magnetic sheet with the parchment side down on top. Rub firmly across the magnetic sheet to make sure the paper is completely adhered.

3 Use a scissors to cut out the frame. Use a craft knife and cutting board/mat to cut out the photo openings. The photo openings may be made into additional magnets by covering them with fabric, brown paper, buttons, etc.

4 Trace the heart pattern to tracing paper, and cut from the fabrics as indicated. Center and glue a heart above and below each frame opening, as shown in the Step 4 illustration. Refer to the photo to glue 3 to 4 buttons randomly on each heart, and 2 buttons evenly spaced between the photo openings.

5 Use the black marking pen to draw short dashed lines around each heart and photo opening. Refer to the photo to draw short perpendicular lines around the frame edges ^{1}/$_4$" (6 mm) apart.

6 Photos should be taped or glued, with acid-free products, from behind the openings in the frame.

Cute as a Button Sampler & Bib

Who's cute as a button? The new baby is, of course. Welcome the little one with this cross-stitch sampler that records all the vital birth statistics—name, date, weight and height. A thoughtful gift paired with the matching bib, the design is accented with real pastel buttons.

List of Materials

For the Set
- 28-count white evenweave fabric, 15" x 18" (38 x 46 cm)
- Premade terrycloth bib with 14-count Aida fabric insert

- 6-strand skeins of DMC embroidery floss in colors listed in Color Key
- No. 24 tapestry needle
- 5/8" (1.5 cm) flat buttons: light blue; white, four each; pink, three

- Frame, your choice
- Pattern Pages 166-167
- Miscellaneous items: scissors, ruler, terrycloth towel, press cloth, iron

1 To stitch each project, refer to the Stitch Charts here and on pages 166-167. Each square on the charts represents 1 square of Aida fabric or 2 threads of evenweave fabric. Symbols correspond to colors in the Color Key.

2 Refer to the Cross-Stitch General Instructions and Stitches on page 160 to work cross-stitches with 2 strands of floss. For the sampler, center and backstitch the name, weight, height and date as indicated on the Sampler Chart using the letters and numbers from the Alphabet/Numbers Chart for your baby's name and statistics. Work backstitches as follows: bow, 1 strand of dark blue (825); name, 2 strands of dark blue (825); remaining lettering, 2 strands of medium cornflower blue (793). Work French knots with 2 strands of floss.

3 To remove wrinkles, place the stitched piece facedown on a terrycloth towel, cover with a damp press cloth and press. To finish, refer to the photo and charts to sew buttons on the stitched piece. Frame the sampler as desired.

Alphabet/Numbers Stitch Chart
1 of 3 (Charts 2 and 3 are on pages 166 & 167)

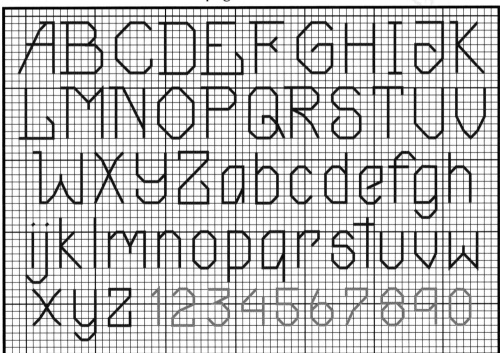

Use 2 strands of Dk. Blue 825 for the baby's name. Use 2 strands of Med. Cornflower Blue 793 for the weight, length and birth date.

Baby Bear Nursery

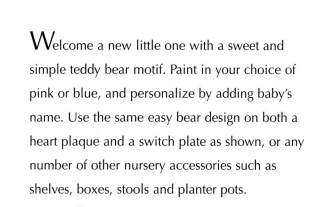

Welcome a new little one with a sweet and simple teddy bear motif. Paint in your choice of pink or blue, and personalize by adding baby's name. Use the same easy bear design on both a heart plaque and a switch plate as shown, or any number of other nursery accessories such as shelves, boxes, stools and planter pots.

List of Materials

- Acrylic paints: titanium (snow) white; raspberry; sapphire; buttermilk; lamp (ebony) black; baby pink; cashmere beige; russet
- Paintbrushes: No. 4 or No. 6 flat; No. 2 round; No. 10/0 liner; 1" (2.5 cm) wash

- Waterbase varnish
- 5³/₄" (14.5 cm) wood heart plaque
- Single switch plate with screws
- Pattern Sheet

- Miscellaneous items: tracing paper, pencil, graphite or transfer paper, stylus, sandpaper, tack cloth, water container, disposable palette, paper towels, sawtooth hanger with nails, hammer, drill with ¹/₁₆" bit, gold wire, wire cutters

1 Refer to Painting Instructions and Techniques on page 156. To prepare the surfaces, sand all the wood pieces to smooth. Use a tack cloth to wipe any dust from the wood.

2 Use the 1" (2.5 cm) wash brush to basecoat all surfaces with 2 coats of baby pink paint. Let dry between coats, paint colors and each step unless otherwise indicated.

3 Trace the patterns to tracing paper. Use graphite paper and a stylus to transfer the pattern to the surface, referring to the photo for placement. Trace only the lettering and the bear outline, not any details at this time.

4 To paint the bear, use the No. 4 or No. 6 flat brush and cashmere beige to basecoat the bear. Transfer all the bear details with graphite paper and stylus. Shade the arms and legs as shown in the photo with russet. Sideload the brush with buttermilk and highlight the top of the ears, face, back, arms and legs. Make small C strokes for the paws. Float raspberry on each cheek, as shown in the Step 4 illustration.

5 Use the liner and black to add the eyes, nose and mouth. Dip the stylus in snow white to dot highlights on eyes, nose and cheeks. Stroke in a few fine lines on paws, body and ears for fur. Use the liner and sapphire to paint the neck bow. Highlight the bow with snow white.

6 Using the handle of the liner brush or the large end of the stylus, add flower trim by dotting 5 buttermilk dots in a circle for each flower. Use the liner and snow white to paint the lettering on the heart plaque.

7 Refer to the photo to drill holes in the top of the heart plaque for the hanger. Insert the wire ends in each hole and twist to secure. Paint the switch plate screws baby pink. Apply a coat of varnish to each project. Let dry.

Noah's Ark Wall Hanging

Noah and his arkful of yo yo animals feel right at home on this whimsical banner riding on a sea of blue felt. But it won't take you 40 days and nights to make, because you just glue premade yo yos to make Noah's cute creatures. Soft felt lends homespun appeal, and wiggle eyes and jewel noses add just the right amount of whimsy.

List of Materials

- Felt: 36" (91.5 cm) denim, 3/4 yd. (0.7 m); cinnamon, 19" x 22" (48.5 x 56 cm); plum, 8" (20.5 cm) square; antique white plush, 4" x 5" (10 x 12.5 cm)
- Backing fabric and fleece or batting, 24" x 27" (61 x 68.5 cm) each
- Fusible web, 2/3 yd. (0.63 m)
- Embroidery floss: ecru; black
- Premade fabric yo yos—see page 161 for instructions on how to make your own and the Yo Yo list on the Pattern Sheet for how many to purchase

- Fabric stiffener
- Wiggle eyes: 7 mm, seven pair; 10 mm, four pair
- Acrylic jewels: 7 mm round ruby, one; 6 mm round black, two; 11 mm faceted black, two
- 5/8" (1.5 cm) plastic rings for hangers
- Pattern Sheet
- Miscellaneous items: tracing paper, pencil, scissors, embroidery needle, hot glue gun, ruler, iron, wax paper, denim quilting thread

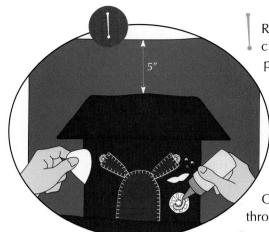

5"

Refer to manufacturer's instructions to iron fusible web to back of cinnamon and plum felt. Trace the patterns and cut out; remove paper backings. Cut a 22" x 25" (56 x 63.5 cm) piece of denim felt. Refer to photo and the Step 1 illustration to place ark on felt 5" (12.5 cm) from top edge; fuse. Fuse Noah's robe and sleeves to ark.

Refer to the Embroidery Stitches on page 159 and the photo to use 2 strands of floss to blanket stitch around ark with black and around Noah's robe and sleeves with ecru. On each sleeve end, blanket stitch through plum felt only; not through the ark.

Glue a Noah hand yo yo just inside each sleeve. Glue beard to bottom half of face yo yo, as shown in the Step 1 illustration. Glue mustache to top of beard and jewel nose and wiggle eyes to face. Glue Noah's head to top of robe and three 1¾" (4.5 cm) ivory yo yos to center of ark bottom.

Refer to the photo and the Wall Hanging Assembly Guide on the Pattern Sheet to make the yo yo animals. After completing each animal, glue on the wiggle eyes and jewel noses, and glue each animal onto the ark. To make each duck, glue a face yo yo to a body yo yo at a slight angle. Fold a beak yo yo in half and glue at inner corners. Glue fold of beak yo yo to center of face yo yo.

To make the lion, overlap and glue 7 mane yo yos around mane center yo yo edge. Fold under edges of head yo yo and glue to form a triangular shape. See the Step 5A illustration. Glue an ear yo yo to wrong side of head, as shown in 5B. Center head and glue on mane. For whiskers, cut 1 strand of embroidery floss into three 2½" (6.5 cm) lengths. Dip floss into fabric stiffener. Remove excess stiffener with fingers. Lay floss on wax paper and let dry for 12 hours. Glue lengths to center of lion's head. Fan whiskers out with finger. To make the lioness, make the lion head and glue to top of body yo yo.

Wrong side   Right side

A   B

For each giraffe, arrange and glue 7 neck yo yos and 1 body yo yo slightly overlapping in a curve, beginning at the top. For giraffe head, turn bottom and top sides of head yo yo under and glue to form a snout and pointed head. Glue to top of neck. Turn edges of ear yo yo under to form a point; glue. Repeat with horn yo yos. Glue ears and horns to head.

To make each cow, turn under opposite edges of a face yo yo and glue. Make ears and horns as for giraffes in Step 6. Glue head to body yo yo. For elephants, glue ear yo yos to each side of a face yo yo. For trunk, overlap and glue 4 trunk yo yos, curving slightly. On the bottom yo yo, glue the last yo yo on it wrong side up. Glue elephants to ark top.

Layer backing fabric right side down, fleece or batting, then banner top. Use denim quilting thread to quilt around ark, elephant and giraffe edges. Trim batting and backing even with banner top. Cut 1" (2.5 cm) denim felt strips and sew ends together to make a continuous 3 yd. (2.75 m) binding strip. Sew binding to banner edge using ¼" (6 mm) seams; do not start strip on a corner. At end of binding, turn under edge and sew. Blind stitch binding strip to back of banner. Sew a plastic ring to each upper back corner.

Li'l Tyke's Messy Mat

Make it pink, blue or a cheery floral, but be sure to make it BIG! Perfect under Baby's high chair to protect carpeting from spilled milk and mushy oatmeal, it folds easily, and it travels in its own carrying case to Grandma's house. The case doubles as a changing pad for those shop 'til you drop trips to the mall. This vinyl-coated spill mat is also a dream come true as Baby grows—it fits perfectly underneath the table or easel for finger-painting, clay and other art projects.

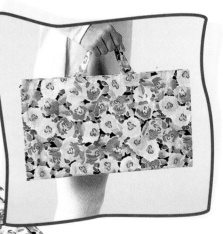

List of Materials

- 45" (115 cm) cotton print fabric, your choice: 1½ yd. (1.4 m) for the mat; ½ yd. (0.5 m) for the carrying case
- 17" (43 cm) clear iron-on vinyl: *matte:* 3 yd. (2.75 m) for the mat; *glossy:* 1⅓ yd. (1.27 m) for the carrying case
- Velcro® adhesive-backed hook and loop tape, ⅝" (1.5 cm) circles, four sets
- Miscellaneous items: scissors, yardstick, straight pins, matching sewing threads, sewing machine, iron

Mat

1 Cut a 33″ x 50″ (84 x 127 cm) fabric piece. Follow manufacturer's instructions to iron vinyl in 2 widthwise strips on the right side of the fabric with ½″ (1.3 cm) overlap.

2 Press a 1″ (2.5 cm) hem twice on each end. Sew hem; use a zigzag stitch, if desired. Repeat for long edges.

Carrying Case

1 Cut an 18″ x 40″ (46 x 102 cm) fabric piece. Fold fabric in half widthwise, right sides together. Leaving a 4″ (10 cm) opening, sew raw edges together using a ½″ (1.3 cm) seam allowance. Clip corners and turn. Slipstitch opening shut.

2 For the handles, cut two 3″ x 12″ (7.5 x 30.5 cm) fabric strips. Fold each strip in half lengthwise, right sides together. Sew long edges using ½″ (1.3 cm) seam allowance; turn. Press strips with seam down center back. Fold and press raw ends to inside.

3 See the Step 3 illustration to pin a handle to case at each end, overlapping edges ¾″ (2 cm). With seam face up, sew handles to inside case. Adhere 8 Velcro circles evenly spaced on long edges.

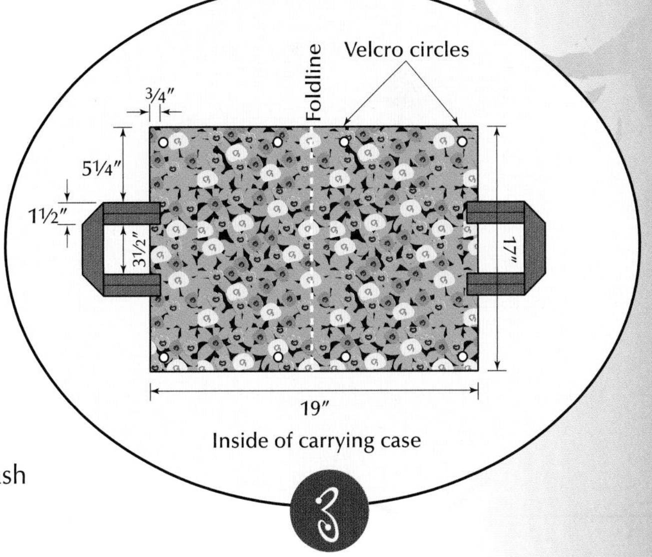

Foldline

Velcro circles

¾″

5¼″

1½″

3½″

17″

19″

Inside of carrying case

3

4 Cut vinyl to fit outside carrying case, then iron vinyl onto fabric.

5 To clean, wipe vinyl with damp cloth; or wash in cold on gentle cycle. Line dry.

Baby Name Blocks

In a different take on ABC blocks, why not make them with the letters of Baby's name? Paint them whatever colors you want—pink for a girl, yellow to match a nursery—then match the satin ribbons and beads. You've got an adorable knickknack that Mom, Dad and Baby will all love to look at. If you get really ambitious, you could make the whole set of 26 for the baby to play with when he or she gets older.

List of Materials

- Drill with ⁹/₁₆" bit
- 1¹/₂" (3.8 cm) wooden blocks, as many as are letters in the child's name
- Medium grit sandpaper, tack cloth
- Royal blue acrylic craft paint
- White stencil paint creme
- Paintbrushes: 1" (2.5 cm) sponge, No. 2 round, ³/₁₆" (4.5 mm) stencil
- 1" (2.5 cm) upper case alphabet stencils
- Matte spray finish

- 1 yd. (0.95 m) each ¹/₄" (6 mm) satin ribbon: yellow, red, blue—this amount will work for 6 letters or less, add ¹/₄ yd. (0.25 m) for each additional letter over 6
- Tapestry needle, big enough for the ribbon to go through
- 5 pearl pony beads, as many as needed to fit between blocks
- Liquid fray preventer
- Miscellaneous items: ruler, pencil, wax paper, paint palette, paper towel, scrap wood or paper, warm water, dish soap

1 Measure to find the center on 2 opposite sides of each block, and mark with a pencil. Drill through from 1 side to the other. To aid in making the hole straight, line the drill up with a wall or other vertical surface, such as shown in the Step 1 illustration. Use some scrap wood to position the block so the drill bit will be on the center mark. Or if you have access to one, use a drill press.

2 Refer to the Painting Instructions and Techniques on page 156. Sand the blocks on all 6 sides, sanding especially well along the edges. Remove the dust with a tack cloth.

3 Lay a piece of wax paper on a flat work surface. Use the sponge brush to basecoat 3 sides of the block with blue. After it is dry to the touch, basecoat the other 3 sides. Repeat to add another coat to all 6 sides. If you should get any rough edges because of dribbles, simply sand them down, remove the dust, and repaint. Continue basecoating until you are satisfied with the coverage.

4 Place the blocks so the drilled sides are facing outwards to the sides; do not stencil the alphabet letters on the sides with the drill holes. Open the stencil creme, and follow the manufacturer's instructions to remove the paint skin with a paper towel. Dip the tip of the stencil brush into the paint and blot the brush onto a paper towel to remove excess paint.

5 Use the stippling technique to practice stenciling some letters on scrap wood or paper. Clean the stencil sheet frequently by scrubbing it with warm water and dish soap. Clean it gently, so you don't tear the stencils. When you are through, clean your brush the same way. Check both the back and front of the sheet to make sure there is no buildup that will rub off onto the blocks.

6 Center the stencil for the first letter onto the block. You may use stencil adhesive to hold it in place, if desired, but the letters are so small, it is really not necessary. Stencil the first letter with white, rotate the block toward you, and stencil the same letter on 1 more side. Repeat to stencil 2 letters on each block, cleaning the stencil sheet after every 2 or 3 letters.

7 Let those letters dry the recommended time following the manufacturer's instructions. When the stencil paint is dry, repeat Step 6 to stencil the other 2 sides. Touch up any white paint dots or smudges by using the round brush to paint over them with the blue background color.

8 Follow the manufacturer's instructions to spray a finish coat on all 6 sides of the blocks, rotating as often as needed. Repeat to add 1 more coat.

9 Thread the 3 ribbons into the tapestry needle. Thread it through the first letter of the name, leaving a 6" (15 cm) tail. Tie an overhand knot on each side of the block to hold it in place. Thread on a pony bead, tie a knot and thread through the second block. Repeat to get all the blocks on the ribbon. Braid 2½" (6.5 cm) on each end of the name, and tie an overhand knot. Trim the ribbon ends as desired. Place some liquid fray preventer on the end of each ribbon.

First Christmas Ornament

For a nontraditional baby gift, try making the infant an ornament for its first Christmas. All will adore the Victorian style with elegant gold ribbon and pearls. Simply purchase a blue ball, blue ribbon roses and pearls, and you've got an ornament for a young boy too.

List of Materials

- 3" (7.5 cm) pink satin Christmas ball with ornament hanger
- 1 yd. (0.95m) each string pearl trims: white oval, pink seed
- Ribbons: 2/3 yd. (0.63 m) pink satin 5/8" (1.5 cm) wide, 2/3 yd. (0.63 m) gold metallic 3/8" (1 cm) wide, 1/4 yd. (0.25 m) gold metallic 1/16" (1.5 mm) wide
- Ribbon flowers: 2 pink satin roses, 4 lace flowers with pink rose centers

- 27 dressmaker pins
- Beads: 4 white seed pearls, five 4 mm white pearl, two 5 mm white pearl, one 5 mm pink flat, one 7 mm pink faceted, one 10 mm oval pearl
- 6" (15 cm) monofilament thread or fishing line
- Fine-line gold metallic pen
- Miscellaneous items: scissors, low-temp hot glue gun, ruler

1 Use a dressmaker's pin to fasten the gold metallic ribbon at the top of ball near the ornament hanger. Wrap the ribbon completely around the ball, pinning it at the bottom and again at the top. Trim the ribbon close to the hanger. Ends do not have to meet, they will be covered by the pink ribbon at the top. Repeat to wrap the gold ribbon again, dividing the ball into quarters.

2 Hot-glue a line along 1 edge of the gold metallic ribbon from top to bottom. Quickly press the white oval string into the glue to make the white pearl border. Repeat this from bottom to top, cutting the pearls at the top. Repeat until the gold metallic ribbon is bordered by string pearls on both sides. You may need to trim the second strings to fit smoothly as they intersect the first strings.

3 See the Step 3 illustration to push 16 dressmaker pins (only a little bit into the ball) for placement of the pink string pearl beads. Cut 4 strands each with 15 pearls and 17 pearls, for a total of 8 strands. Hot-glue near 1 of the top pins, and quickly press the end pearl of a 15-pearl strand in the glue. Remove and discard the pin. Repeat to glue the opposite end of the strand, as shown in the illustration. Repeat to glue a 17-pearl strand at the lower pins. Repeat to glue the remaining strands around the ball.

4 Place each of the 4 white pearl seed beads on a dressmaker's pin. Insert each pin through a lace flower in the center of the rose. Refer to the photo to position a lace flower in each quarter between the pink seed pearls and the ornament top.

5 Tie a knot in 1 end of the monofilament line to make the dangling tail. Thread the beads as shown in the photo: 5 mm pink flat, 10 mm oval pearl, two 4 mm white pearls, 7 mm pink faceted, and three 4 mm white pearls. Add a dot of hot glue to the bottom bead to better hold the knot. Knot the top of the dangling tail, and cut it off; hot-glue it to the bottom of the ornament. Hot-glue the two 5 mm white pearls to the bottom of the ornament, 1 on each side of the dangling tail.

6 Thread the 1/16" (1.5 mm) gold ribbon through the ornament hanger for a hanging loop, letting it hang open to both sides for now. Cut 12" (30.5 cm) of the pink satin ribbon, and fold it into a 4-loop bow as shown in the Step 6A illustration. Hot-glue the loops in place, and the bow to the top of the ornament. Take the hanging loop and tie a knot, squeezing the pink bow together in the center, as shown in 6B. Tie the hanging loop ribbon ends together in a small bow.

7 Cut two 4" (10 cm) pieces of pink satin ribbon; cut V's in 1 end of each. Use the gold metallic marker to write the baby's name on 1 ribbon, and the birth date on the other. Hot-glue the straight edge of each ribbon to the ornament under the bow, so the ribbons hang on opposite sides. Hot-glue the 2 satin roses as shown in the photo, 1 on each side of the top pink bow.

b a b i e s

Tote/Diaper Bag

This colorful yet practical canvas bag has a parade of baby animals and letters marching across the side. Fill it with diapers, wipes, clothes and toys for a wonderful shower gift! You'll have loads of fun creating this with rubber stamps and paint. It's easy to do, even for beginners.

List of Materials

- Natural canvas tote with pockets, 19" x 12" x 4" (48.5 x 30.5 x 10 cm)*

- Rubber Stampede Decorative Stamps: chick, bunny, lamb, butterfly, and 3" (7.5 cm) alphabet*

- Rubber Stampede Decorative™ Stamping Paint: ivory, white, lavender, jade, bittersweet orange, straw, Indiana rose, denim blue, blue jay, fuchsia*

- Rubber Stampede Applicator Sponges*

- Brushes: No. 2 flat and round

- 3/4" (2 cm) painter's masking tape

- Miscellaneous items: ruler, paper or scrap fabric, paper towels or cloth, disposable palette

*(See Sources on page 175 for purchasing information.)

1 See the Step 1 illustration to tape off 4 rectangles, 3″ (7.5 cm) wide and 3³⁄₈″ (8.5 cm) high, across the top of the bag above the pocket. Tape off 5³⁄₈″ (13.5 cm) high rectangles across the bottom, with the following widths: bunny 4¹⁄₂″ (11.5 cm), lamb 4⁵⁄₈″ (11.7 cm), and chick 3¹⁄₂″ (9 cm).

2 Refer to the Painting Instructions and Techniques on page 156. Let colors dry completely before adding more coats or additional colors.

3 Basecoat the masked-off squares as shown in the photo and the Step 1 illustration: top row, left to right, lavender, straw, Indiana rose, and jade; bottom row: jade, Indiana rose, lavender. Mix each paint color on the palette with white to make it more pastel and use an applicator sponge to dab on the paint. Test the sponge on paper or scrap fabric first to get the feel for how much paint to use. Let dry; do not remove tape.

4 Test each stamp on paper or scrap fabric first to get the feel for how much paint to use. Apply paints evenly to the stamps with a sponge. Wipe off paints after each use with a paper towel or cloth. Do not roll the stamp when pressing it onto the bag.

5 Refer to the photo to see which way to angle the letter and animal stamps. For the letters, do not mix white with the colors. Apply fuchsia paint to the letter B stamp. Stamp on the lavender rectangle in the top row. Wipe off the stamp, and stamp a lavender B in the pink rectangle. Stamp the A with denim blue and the Y with blue jay. Remove all tape.

6 Apply ivory paint on the bunny stamp, and stamp the image onto the green rectangle. Using the flat brush, apply more ivory to completely coat the bunny. Mix a little fuchsia and white paint on the palette, and shade under and around the nose, ears, bottom of the legs and tail. Use the round brush to outline and add detail lines with straight fuchsia, as shown in the photo.

7 Apply white paint on the lamb stamp, and stamp the image onto the pink rectangle. Using the flat brush, apply more white to completely coat the lamb. Mix a little lavender and white paint, and shade under and around the face, neck, legs and tummy. Use the round brush to outline and add detail lines with straight lavender, as shown in the photo.

8 Mix a little straw and white paint on the palette; apply the mix on the chick stamp, and stamp the image onto the lavender rectangle. Using the flat brush, apply more paint to completely coat the chick. Shade under and around the face, tummy, tail and wings with straight straw. Use the round brush to add bittersweet orange beak and feet, as shown in the photo. Dot a blue jay eye.

9 Stamp the butterflies as shown in the photo, using the following colors. Use the flat brush to shade the inner wings as follows. Use the round brush to paint over the antennae and make the wing dots as follows:

Body Basecoat	Jade + White	Blue Jay
Antennae Basecoat	Jade	Blue Jay
Wing Basecoat	Straw	Fuchsia
Inner Wing Shading	Orange	Lavender
Wing Dots	Denim Blue	Lavender

Graduation

Graduating is an accomplishment that deserves more than just
a document. Honor the graduate with handmade giftwrap,
decorations, memory makers and useful tools. After all, graduation
not only marks the end of an era—it's also a new beginning.

Tassel Grad

Tassels are to graduation as cake is to a wedding. We've come up with a novel grad, ecstatic as can be, who's sure to make a hit at a party, on a gift, dangling from a car mirror or trimming a photo of your favorite grad. Buy supplies for more than one because you'll want to make a dozen!

List of Materials

- Natural wood shapes: 3/4" (2 cm) bead; 3/8" (1 cm) beads, two; 3/8" (1 cm) dowel, 2" (5 cm) length

- Black foam or felt, 1" (2.5 cm) square

- Acrylic paints: black; white; medium pink

- Clear monofilament, 1 yd. (0.95 m)

- 4" (10 cm) black fringe, 5" (12.5 cm)

- Gold embroidery floss, 6" (15 cm)

- Fine gold wire, 1" (2.5 cm)

- Paintbrushes: liner; small flat

- Tools: small drill and bit; small clamp or vise

- Miscellaneous items: scissors, ruler, 1 1/4" (3.2 cm) square white paper, pencil, sandpaper, straight pin

1. Drill vertical and horizontal holes through center of the dowel, as shown in the Step 3 illustration. Sand ends of dowel to slightly round them.

2. Paint the dowel black. See the Step 3 illustration to paint top of head bead black. Use liner brush and black to paint the mouth. Paint eyes white; let dry. Paint black pupils with white highlights. Use medium pink to paint cheeks and nose dots as shown.

3. To assemble the doll, use 18″ (46 cm) length of monofilament and see the Step 3 illustration. For the arms/hands, thread one 3/8″ (1 cm) bead centered on monofilament. Knot ends tightly around bead. Thread both ends lengthwise through the dowel. Thread 1 end through second 3/8″ (1 cm) bead; knot ends tightly around bead. Clip ends to 3/8″ (1 cm) and thread back through bead hole.

18″ piece for hat/ head/ body

18″ piece for arms/hands

3″

3

4. Fold remaining monofilament in half. To make hanging loop, knot together 3″ (7.5 cm) from folded end. Enlarge knot by tying a second knot on top of the first. Make a tiny hole in center of the foam square hat and thread ends through to the knot. Slip both ends through the head and down through center of the arms. Tie a knot at bottom large enough so it will not slip back through. Clip off excess.

5. For the diploma, roll paper tightly and twist gold wire around center. Hot glue to end of bead hand, covering monofilament ends.

6. For the robe, begin at 1 side of the fringe and roll tightly and glue along the upper end. Glue top of rolled fringe to bottom center of dowel, covering the knot.

7. To make the gold floss hat tassel, fold floss in half. Knot 1/2″ (1.3 cm) from fold to make loop. Trim ends to 1/2″ (1.3 cm). Use pin to separate floss strands to fluff. Wrap loop around hanger on hat top; apply dot of glue to secure. Glue tassel knot to edge of hat.

Rubber Stamp Congrats for Grads

Honor graduates with a card and gift wrap set made just for them! Whether your graduate is leaving high school, college or graduate school, we've got the card and gift bag set that's just right! Just stamp, emboss and stencil . . . and your well wishes are ready for that special day!

List of Materials

- ¹/₂" (1.3 cm) adhesive-backed foam circles*, one package
- White matte notecard and envelope
- 4¹/₄" (10.8 cm) square black card stock
- Black matte gift bag
- White tissue paper

- Rubber stamps*: Congratulations; star
- Opaque pigment stamp pads*: gold and black
- Embossing gun*
- Tangerine dual tip embossing pen*
- Embossing powders*: gold and sparkle rainbow

- Tassel in your choice of school colors
- White craft glue
- Miscellaneous items: ruler, scissors, craft knife

*(See Sources on pg. 175 for purchasing information.)

1 To stamp, press the rubber stamp firmly and evenly onto the stamp pad, then firmly and evenly onto the paper. Do not roll the stamp pad when pressing it on the paper or pad. Reink the stamp after each use.

2 When you are embossing images, a special slow-drying ink is used. An embossing pen can be used in place of an inked image when you want to color in a large area or free-hand draw an image to be embossed. To emboss, generously cover the wet inked image with embossing powder. Shake off excess powder onto a clean sheet of paper so it can be saved for reuse. Apply heat with an embossing gun over the image to melt the powder, creating a shiny, raised look; see the Step 2 illustration. A toaster or iron can be used instead of an embossing gun by holding paper above the heat source. Be careful not to burn the paper.

3 Refer to the photo and use the black pigment ink pad and sparkle rainbow embossing powder to stamp and emboss "Congratulations" images on the card front, stamping off paper where needed.

4 Color balloons and confetti with tangerine embossing pen. Emboss in gold. Rule lines around edges of card with embossing pen and emboss in gold.

5 Write "Graduate" on black square with embossing pen and emboss in gold; see the Step 2 illustration. Stamp and emboss stars around edges using gold pigment stamp pad and gold embossing powder.

6 Attach mortarboard to card, sandwiching foam circles between layers to give the hat dimension. Attach foam circle "button," and glue tassel to the mortarboard as shown.

7 For the envelope, use the embossing pen to rule lines around entire envelope and flap. Emboss in gold. Stamp and emboss stars in gold.

8 For the bag, stamp and emboss stars on bag with gold pigment stamp and gold embossing powder.

9 For the tissue, refer to Steps 3 and 4 to stamp and emboss "Congratulations" over entire tissue. Color and emboss balloons with embossing pen and gold embossing powder.

School Days Autograph Pencil

Create a wonderful keepsake of those memorable school years with this giant-sized wooden pencil. Now, and years from now, the signatures and comments of friends are sure to bring a smile. Add the school's name, a bow in school colors and a wire hanger, then give it to your favorite graduate to collect school chums' autographs.

List of Materials

- 3/16" (4.5 mm) balsa wood, 4" x 36" (10 x 91.5 cm)
- Acrylic paints: true apricot; medium apricot; dusty peach; dusty beige; dusty grey; silver
- Paintbrushes: 3/4" (2 cm) flat; Nos. 2 and 4 shader; 1" (2.5 cm) sponge
- All-purpose primer
- Gloss varnish
- Fine-point black permanent marker
- Painter's masking paper
- 19-gauge black wire, 18" (46 cm)
- 1/8" (3 mm) satin ribbon in school colors, 1½ yd. (1.4 m) each
- Pattern Sheet
- Miscellaneous items: tracing paper, graphite paper, masking tape, pencil, stylus, yardstick, craft knife, drill, fine sandpaper, tack cloth, disposable palette, water basin, paper towels, wirecutters, toothpick, hot glue gun

1 Refer to Painting Instructions & Techniques on page 156. Trace the patterns, position and tape them on the wood, using the yardstick to complete the sides of the pencil for a total length of 36″ (91.5 cm). Use the stylus and graphite paper to transfer the patterns to the wood, omitting the dashed lines. Use the stylus to gently press over the detail lines on the metal band section below the eraser, slightly indenting the wood.

2 Use the craft knife to cut out the wooden pencil shape; sand lightly. Drill holes in the eraser. Apply a coat of primer and let dry. Sand lightly.

3 Paint the middle section of the pencil with true apricot, on the front, sides and back of pencil. Let dry between paint colors, coats and each step. To make the 5 vertical lines on the middle section designating the beveled sides of a pencil, mark both ends of the dashed pattern lines on each unpainted end for placement. Starting on the left side, place a strip of masking paper the length of the middle section, connecting the corresponding marks on each end.

4 Wet and blot the 3/4″ (2 cm) flat brush. Load 1 side of the brush with medium apricot. With the paint-loaded side on the edge of the masking paper, pull the brush down the length of the masking paper, as shown in the Step 4 illustration. Remove the masking paper and, using a clean strip for each line, repeat to paint 4 more vertical lines.

5 Paint the pencil as follows: point end, dusty beige; lead, dusty grey and silver mix; eraser, dusty peach highlighted with a few light strokes of medium apricot; metal band, silver. Use the dusty grey/silver mix to brush lightly over the horizontal lines and to paint every other vertical stripe on the metal band; see the Step 5 illustration.

6 Use the black marker to write the school name and room number across the top of the metal band. Apply a coat of varnish.

7 For the hanger, twist the wire around a pencil to curl it. Insert 2″ (5 cm) of each end through the holes from the back. Wrap each end around a toothpick to curl; glue wire in back.

8 Cut an 8″ (20.5 cm) length of 1 ribbon color. Make a multi-loop bow with remaining ribbon and tie at center with the 8″ (20.5 cm) length. Trim the ends and glue the bow to the eraser at the upper left.

Candle Cup Graduate

Diploma in hand, this miniature graduate is all smiles because she's made it! Personalize your graduates by substituting a different hair color or style, and by painting them with school colors. Then use them in all sorts of ways: for a graduation open house, as cake toppers or package tie-ons, or as shelf sitters and party favors.

List of Materials

For Each Graduate
- Wooden shapes: 1³/₈" (3.5 cm) candle cup; 1¹/₄" (3.2 cm) head bead; ¹/₁₆" x 1¹/₂" (1.5 mm x 3.8 cm) square, one each
- Acrylic paints: blue; peach
- Rayon embroidery floss: royal blue (30797); light blue (30813)

- ¹/₈" (3 mm) light blue satin ribbon, 6" (15 cm)
- Doll hair, your choice
- Blue chenille stem
- 7 mm black wiggle eyes, one pair
- Hot glue gun with needlenose nozzle and wood glue sticks

- Miscellaneous items: typing paper, ruler, small paintbrush, disposable palette, scissors, wire cutters, fine-point black permanent marking pen, air-soluble marker, powdered cosmetic blush, cotton swab, transparent tape

1 Paint the candle cup body and wood square mortarboard blue. Paint the head bead peach. Let dry.

2 Glue the head to the top of the candle cup. For arms, cut a 4" (10 cm) chenille stem length; glue the center of the stem to the upper back of the body. Shape the arms.

3 Arrange and glue hair on top of the head as desired.

4 For the tassel, cut one 4¹/2" (11.5 cm) length of royal blue floss and two 4¹/2" (11.5 cm) lengths of light blue floss. Align the ends and fold in half. Wrap one 4" (10 cm) strand of royal blue floss around the folded tassel end and tie a double knot. Trim floss ends even. Glue the tassel to the top of the mortarboard. Glue the mortarboard on top of the head.

5 Use the air-soluble marker and refer to the photo to draw the mouth. Trace over the mouth with the black pen. Glue the eyes to the face. Use the cotton swab to lightly blush the cheeks as shown in the Step 5 illustration.

6 Cut a 1¹/4" x 2" (3.2 x 5 cm) piece of white paper, roll it into a small scroll and tape the edge. Wrap one 4" (10 cm) strand of royal blue floss around the scroll and double knot. Glue the scroll to the end of 1 arm.

7 Tie a small ribbon bow and glue to the center front of the graduate.

Hats off to Grads

College-bound or in the work force, high school graduates become instant celebrities. Their fans send cards and gifts, throw parties in their honor and snap their photo at every opportunity. So for your favorite grad, why not fuse hats cut from lamé to embellish a T-shirt, invitation and congratulatory card.

List of Materials

For Each Project
- Lamé, 3 assorted colors, scraps or 1/8 yd. (.15 m) each
- 1/4 yd. (0.25 m) low-temp fusible web
- Iridescent dimensional squeeze-tip paints, your choice of colors
- Iridescent glitter

For Shirt
- White T-shirt

For Card & Invitation
- 4 1/4" x 5 1/2" (10.8 x 14 cm) white note cards, two
- Felt-tip markers, your choice of colors

- Pattern Page 171
- Miscellaneous items: white craft glue, pencil, ruler, scissors, tracing paper, T-shirt board, 1 1/2" x 3" (3.8 x 7.5 cm) cardboard, masking tape, iron

Preparation

1. Follow the manufacturer's instructions to fuse web to the lamé, keeping iron on as low a temperature as possible. Test a scrap of lamé first, before doing the hats.

2. Trace the patterns onto tracing paper, then onto the paper backing of the fusible web, as instructed on the patterns. For the card also draw a 1″ x 3½″ (2.5 x 9 cm) strip. Cut out the appliqués and follow the instructions for each of the projects.

Shirt

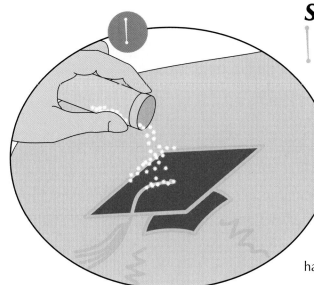

1. Wash and dry shirt to remove sizing; do not use fabric softener. Refer to the photo for placement and fuse hats to upper half of shirt front. Let them cool. Tape the shirt tightly over the T-shirt board. Using dimensional paint, outline each hat and refer to the photo to paint a tassel flowing from each hat center. Also paint squiggles randomly on the shirt. Sprinkle paint with glitter while still wet, as shown in the Step 1 illustration. To launder shirt, hand wash in warm water with mild detergent and hang to dry.

Card & Invitation

1. To make the card, angle strip in lower right corner of note card. Trim edges even with card as shown in the Step 1 illustration. Fuse strip to card, then hat overlapping strip. To make the invitation, cut 3 small hats from lamé and fuse to left note card edge.

2. Use markers and refer to the photo to print messages on the invitation and card. Outline lamé with dimensional paint, adding tassels flowing from each hat center. Also paint small squiggles on invitation. Sprinkle with glitter while paint is still wet.

Tutti-Frutti Beverage Set

To launch them into independence, graduates need some gifts that haven't come from a garage sale or Grandma's attic. A painted festive beverage set will allow your recipient to serve cool drinks in cool style.

List of Materials

- Glass pitcher with matching drink glasses
- Surface cleaner/conditioner
- Air-dry enamel paints: apple candy green; ultra white; fuchsia; azure blue; citrus yellow; tangerine

- Air-dry enamel gloss finish
- Sponges: compressed craft sheet; natural sea
- No. 1 liner paintbrush
- Pattern Page 171

- Miscellaneous items: tracing paper, pencil, stylus, scissors, container of water, paper towels, ruler; 1/2" (1.3 cm) masking tape, disposable palette, sponge brush

1   Trace the patterns from the pattern page and cut them out. Dip the compressed sponges into a container of water to expand; squeeze them with paper towels to remove the water.

2   To prepare the glassware for painting, refer to the manufacturer's instructions to brush the surface cleaner/conditioner on the outside of the glass. The paints are nontoxic but are not recommended for use on surfaces with direct food contact.

3   To paint each glass, apply masking tape around the top, center and bottom of the glass to divide it into top and bottom sections. Mix equal parts of apple candy green and ultra white paint. Lightly dip the square sponge into the mixture. Blot paint on a paper towel each time the sponge is loaded with paint. Refer to the photo to press the square onto the top and bottom halves of the glass. Let dry between paint colors and each step. Rinse the sponge, squeeze dry and dip it into unmixed apple candy green. Refer to the photo to sponge overlapping squares onto the glass.

4   On the opposite side of the top and bottom halves of the glass, follow Step 3 to sponge azure blue squares overlapped by fuchsia squares, as shown in the Step 4 illustration.

5   Between the sets of squares, sponge tangerine fruit slices, then citrus yellow fruit slices on the opposite sides. Reverse the colors to sponge a center and sections onto the fruit slices. Use the liner brush to paint the outer rind.

6   Remove the masking tape. Use the liner to paint a wavy azure blue line, then a wavy fuchsia line around the center of the glass. Use the stylus or end of the paintbrush handle to make random 3-dot clusters of apple candy green, tangerine and citrus yellow on the glass.

7   Use the sea sponge to apply 1 coat of gloss finish to the entire outer surface.

8   To paint the pitcher, follow Steps 3-5 to tape and paint overlapping squares and alternating fruit slices. Sponge the sets of squares with azure blue and fuchsia, tangerine and citrus yellow, or apple candy green and the green mixture. Sponge the fruit slices with citrus yellow and apple candy green, tangerine and citrus yellow, or apple candy green and the green mixture.

9   Remove the tape. Refer to the photo to paint 3 sets of wavy lines: apple candy green and the green mixture at the top; azure blue and fuchsia at the center; citrus yellow and tangerine at the bottom. Paint side-by-side wavy tangerine and apple candy green lines down the outer edge of the pitcher handle. Follow Step 6 to paint dot clusters on the pitcher and handle. Follow Step 7 to apply gloss finish.

Painted Popcorn Keeper

Every graduate needs to eat to keep going, whether at school or work. And what better quick and easy meal—although maybe not the most nutritious—than microwave popcorn? Even better, the delicious smell is guaranteed to bring other people running, which means lots of new friends.

List of Materials

- 5¹⁄₂″ x 7¹⁄₄″ x 12″ (14 x 18.7 x 30.5 cm) wooden popcorn keeper*
- Wood sealer
- Acrylic paints: soft beige; dusty beige; dusty mauve; deep mauve; dusty green; deep green; dusty lavender; black
- Paintbrushes: No. 1 script liner; No. 12 flat synthetic; 1″ and 2″ (2.5 and 5 cm) sponge; 1″ (2.5 cm) synthetic bristle
- ³⁄₄″ (2 cm) Scotch™ Magic™ tape

- Kneadable eraser
- Matte waterbase varnish
- Pattern Sheet
- Miscellaneous items: 400 and 600 grit wet and dry sandpaper, tack cloth, pencil, stylus, tracing paper, graphite paper, masking tape, palette knife, disposable palette, paper towels, water basin, brown paper bag; *optional:* wood filler, cardboard, credit card

*(See Sources on pg. 175 for purchasing information.)

1 Refer to Painting General Instructions and Techniques on page 156. Sand the surface and remove dust with tack cloth. Seal the wood following manufacturer's instructions. Basecoat the front of the box with soft beige, the sides and back with dusty mauve, the lid with dusty green and the knob with dusty beige. Let dry between paint colors, coats and each step.

2 Refer to photo to paint the plaid design on the box front. Beginning 1/4" (6 mm) from the left side of the box front, apply 3/4" (2 cm) tape vertically from top to bottom. Firmly secure the edges by rubbing with a fingernail or credit card. Place a second length of tape on the right edge of the first piece and press lightly in place. Place a third piece of tape to the right of the second, pressing firmly. Remove the second piece and place it on the right edge of the third piece, pressing lightly. Apply a fourth piece of tape, pressing firmly. Remove the second piece and move it to the right edge of the fourth piece. Using piece number 2 as a spacer, continue in this manner to apply strips of tape to cover the front of the box. There will be a strip of exposed paint between each piece of tape. Paint alternating dusty mauve and dusty green vertical stripes. Let dry. Remove tape.

3 Repeat Step 2 to tape the box front horizontally, beginning at the top. Paint the horizontal stripes with a dusty beige wash. Let dry. Remove tape.

4 Mix equal parts of dusty mauve and deep mauve to make dark mauve. Mix equal parts of dusty green and deep green to make dark green. Thin paints to an ink-like consistency.

5 Using the liner brush, see the Step 5 illustration to paint dark mauve vertical lines on both sides of the dusty mauve stripes. Paint dark green vertical lines on both sides of the dusty green stripes. Paint double lines at the top and a single line at the bottom of each horizontal dusty beige stripe using dark mauve.

6 Refer to the Step 6 illustration to paint a dusty lavender vertical line near the right side of each vertical stripe. Paint a dusty lavender horizontal line near the bottom of each soft beige horizontal stripe.

7 Paint vertical and horizontal lines with dusty beige through each horizontal and vertical soft beige stripe.

8 Trace the lettering pattern; use the stylus and graphite paper to transfer the pattern to the front of the popcorn keeper. Use the liner brush and black to paint the lettering, applying pressure on the brush to paint the wider areas and releasing pressure to paint the thinner areas. Let dry.

9 Wipe with the tack cloth. Apply varnish in long, smooth and slightly overlapping strokes. Check corners and edges to catch drips. Apply 2 to 3 additional coats, allowing each coat to dry completely; a wet coat on top of a partially dried coat can result in tears in the lower layers of varnish. Rub the surface lightly with a piece of brown paper bag between coats to smooth. Wipe with the tack cloth.

10 Sand the final coat with 600 grit wet and dry sandpaper with a little water sprinkled on the surface. The water serves as a lubricant that allows smooth sanding without scratching the final coat. To clean the surface, use a damp sponge and a gentle soap.

Dorm-Savvy Bath Tote

Whether the grad is heading for dorm life or her first apartment, a shared bathroom calls for an innovative "storage and transport" system. This colorful personalized tote fills the bill, and it's a snap to create.

List of Materials

- Plastic tote or bucket with sturdy handle and ample room for storing toiletry items
- Opaque paint markers in assorted colors
- Discarded plastic container, such as a milk jug, for practicing paint designs
- Goo Gone® for removing wet paint mistakes

- Toiletry items, such as shampoo, conditioner, shower gel and nylon scrub puff, shaving lotion and razor, toothpaste and toothbrush, soap, wash cloths
- Miscellaneous items: paper, scissors, pencil, tape

1 Wash the tote to remove any fingerprints or oily residue; wipe dry.

2 Plan out the placement of your design on paper. Tape the design to the side of the tote to check the fit.

3 Test the paint markers on the side of a discarded plastic container, such as a milk jug, to get the feel for how the markers work, the amount of pressure to use, and the angle at which to hold them. Try letters, dots, squiggles, or bubbles, following the design in the photo or making up your own.

4 Paint the design on the tote, beginning with the lettering, and using your paper design as a guide. Refer to the Step 4 illustration and the photo for making "dotted" letters. Allow the paint to dry completely before painting over any areas with another color.

5 If you make any mistakes while painting, remove the wet paint with Goo Gone, swab the area with a clean dry cloth, and repaint. Allow the design to dry completely.

6 Fill the tote with toiletry items in an array of colors to complement the paint colors used on the tote.

Collaged CD Holder

Right up there with a graduate's prized belongings, after the TV and computer, is the musical system with its collection of CDs. You will go to the top of the class by creating a personalized storage system out of magazine pictures and photos of family and friends. If ever the student becomes homesick, all he or she has to do is put on some tunes while looking at memories from home.

List of Materials

- CD holder, 14" x 7" x 5½" (35.5 x 18 x 14 cm) shown in photo. Any size will work, side surfaces should be plastic or wood, something that is not too slick and can be sanded. Metal would not be a good surface choice.
- Sandpaper, medium or rough grit
- 1" (2.5 cm) sponge brush

- Plaid® Mod Podge®, matte finish
- Colored paper or wrapping paper, two 16" x 9" (40.5 x 23 cm) pieces or enough to cover the 2 flat sides of your CD holder
- Blank or unwanted CD, use 1 of the many online free disk offers that abound

- 10-12 color photocopies of photos of family and friends
- 2-3 current popular magazines with much advertising
- Miscellaneous items: paper towels, wax paper, pencil, scissors—regular and decorative edge, scrap paper

1. Use a piece of sandpaper to rough up both surface sides of the CD holder. Sand until you can feel a definite roughness when rubbing your fingers along the side. Wipe off the dust with a damp paper towel; let dry. Place wax paper down on a flat work surface that will give you plenty of working space around the CD holder. Use the sponge brush to apply a basecoat of Mod Podge to both sides, and let dry.

2. Lay the colored or wrapping paper pieces wrong side up on a flat surface. This paper will be the background for the collage of photos and images. Place the CD holder flat on its side and trace around the side. See the Step 2 illustration to trace the other side of the CD holder on the other piece of colored or wrapping paper.

Wrong side of background paper

Wrong side of background paper

3. Cut out both pieces of paper, and place them on the CD holder to check the fit. Trim any edges as necessary. Use the sponge brush to apply a coat of Mod Podge to the CD holder. Place the paper on the holder, and smooth the paper in place with your fingers. If desired, you could use the brush to smooth the paper, and place another layer of Mod Podge over the entire paper. Let dry, and repeat on the other side of the CD holder.

4. Repeat Step 2 to trace the CD holder sides onto some scrap paper; you can use this to lay out the collage. Select words, images and photos from the magazines, and from your collection of color photocopies. Begin to trim and cut them out to fit the background area; refer to the photo for ideas. Use a straight edge scissors and cut along image outlines, or tear the paper for a natural look. Or you can use decorative edge scissors in the many patterns available. Also lay out items on the blank CD.

5. Lay the CD holder flat on 1 side. Begin gluing the bottommost layer of images in the collage. Place the items right side down on the wax paper. Use the sponge brush to apply Mod Podge to the back of an item, and place it on the CD holder. Smooth out air bubbles with your fingers or the brush. Repeat to glue all the images on the 1 side, replacing the wax paper gluing sheet as often as necessary to avoid getting Mod Podge on the front of the images.

6. When gluing images to the CD, wipe off any excess Mod Podge immediately to avoid clouding the shiny surface. Do not glue the CD onto the holder yet, let it dry separately.

7. When your collage is complete on 1 side, apply an even coat of Mod Podge to the entire surface for a finish coat; let dry. Repeat Steps 5 and 7 on the opposite side. When completely dry, use the Mod Podge to adhere the CD to the side.

For Loads of Laundry

A sure sign of growing up and moving out is having to do laundry on your own! Because this is not a chore that gets done very often, a large laundry bag is the ideal gift for a graduate to store those dirty clothes in an apartment or dorm that is short on space. Personalize the laundry bag by dyeing it with school or favorite colors.

List of Materials

- Rit® dye, 1 box each, 1 1/8 oz. (31.9 g): #46 periwinkle blue and #19 mauve
- 24" x 36" (61 x 91.5 cm) white nylon laundry bag
- Miscellaneous items: Dutch oven, stovetop, water, rubber bands in different sizes, tongs, kitchen sink, scissors

1. Follow the manufacturer's instructions to use the Stove Top Technique to heat the water and make the periwinkle dye in a Dutch oven.

2. Prepare the laundry bag for dyeing by twisting it tightly lengthwise into a long tube. Tie it into knots and wrap rubber bands around it. The more twists and knots, the more interesting textures you will get when dyeing. Where the fabric is tightly twisted, knotted or banded the fabric will stay white, as the dye will not get through there. You do want to leave several areas undyed, so they can be dyed mauve in the next steps.

3. When the laundry bag looks like a gnarled ball, carefully place it in the pot of simmering dye. Stir the water, and turn the bag often with tongs, for about 30 min. Carry the pot to the sink, and remove the laundry bag with tongs or a large spoon. Place it in the sink. Pour the dye out of the pot carefully down the drain (very carefully if you have a white porcelain sink).

4. Repeat Step 1 to make a batch of mauve dye. When the dye is just coming to a simmer, begin to rinse the laundry bag in cold water until the water runs clear. Leave it knotted at first, then remove all the knots and rubber bands and rinse until clear.

5. Repeat Steps 2 and 3 to twist and dye the laundry bag mauve, keeping in mind that you do want some areas of the bag to stay white; see the Step 5 illustration. Repeat Step 4 to rinse out the bag. Hang up over a laundry tub or outside to dry.

GARDEN ANGEL

ONLY GOD CAN MAKE
FLOWERS AND TREES
BUT HE PUT ME IN
CHARGE OF
SEEDS AND WEEDS

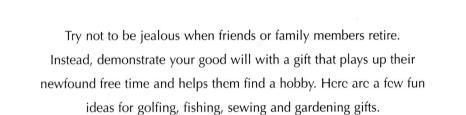

Retirement

Try not to be jealous when friends or family members retire. Instead, demonstrate your good will with a gift that plays up their newfound free time and helps them find a hobby. Here are a few fun ideas for golfing, fishing, sewing and gardening gifts.

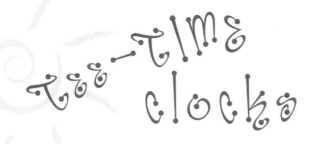

tee-time clocks

Golfers rarely need to be reminded of a tee-time, but a whimsical clock like either of these two is really the perfect gift for a retiring duffer. Using an inexpensive wooden case clock, either can be made quickly and cheaply in hours. It will be a conversation piece for years to come and remind the retiree to call his or her still-slaving coworkers for coffee every once in a while.

List of Materials

- Plain wooden case desk clock
- Drill and 5/32" drill bit
- Masking tape
- 25 to 30 colored golf tees
- Rubber mallet
- Wood glue, optional

1 Mark desired placement of tees on clock face, sides, and top, using a pencil. Placement may be random as in the rectangular blonde clock, or uniformly spaced, as in the semicircle teak clock. For uniform tee placement, use a measuring tape or ruler to evenly mark along the edge. If embellishing a wall clock, you may want to put some tees in the bottom as well.

2 See the Step 2 illustration to wrap a piece of masking tape around drill bit with edge of tape 3/8″ (1 cm) from tip of bit. A piece of masking tape placed on the clock at the location to be drilled will prevent possible splintering at edges of drill holes, if that is a problem with the type of wood clock you choose.

Tape

3 Drill holes at each marked point, varying the angles of the holes. Stop drilling each hole when edge of tape meets surface of wood.

4 Insert tees in holes. Gently tap tees with rubber mallet to secure them. If tees are loose, secure them in holes using wood glue. Multicolored tees work well with the haphazard design; traditional white or a single color is better with an orderly design. Use acrylic paint to paint the tees before insertion, if you're looking for that perfect color. The new longer tees will also add an extra design element to a clock, by protruding out farther than standard tees. Try some of those to achieve a pattern or even more eclectic look. Monogrammed golf balls and tools for monogramming are available in sports stores or specialty gift catalogs.

Golf Goodie Box

For many people, retirement means only one thing—more time to golf. For some poor souls it is finally having the chance to learn how to play golf for the first time. If your retiring coworker fits either description, here is a gift he or she will be sure to love. Pack it full of useful golf goodies, such as tees, gloves, balls, score cards, divot repair tools or even a gift certificate to the local pro shop!

List of Materials

- 5¹/₂" x 7¹/₂" x 3" (14 x 19.3 x 7.5 cm) oval papier-mâché box
- 8" x 9" (20.5 x 23 cm) mat board
- Green spray paint
- 1 or 2 golf magazines, golf scorecards, golf photos, etc.

- Paintbrushes: old one for applying glue, sponge or medium flat
- Spray acrylic finish
- White acrylic paint
- 1 golf ball
- 2 golf tees

- Pattern Sheet
- Miscellaneous items: tracing paper, pencil, masking tape, craft knife, cutting surface, scissors, white craft glue, wax paper, hardcover books, paper plate or bowl, hot glue gun

1. Trace hat brim pattern onto tracing paper. If your box is a slightly different size than that in the project, you can make your own pattern. Simply place the box onto the mat board and trace around the bottom of the box. Then freehand draw a brim that will extend on 1 side, that is approximately 3" (7.5 cm) deep in the center.

2. Place the traced pattern upside down onto the back side of the mat board, and tape. Trace the back side of the pattern with the pencil, transferring the pattern lines to the mat board. Use a craft knife to cut out the hat brim on a cutting surface, or use scissors.

3. Place a piece of wax paper on a flat work surface. Apply white craft glue to the bottom of the oval box, and set it on top of the mat board hat brim on the wax paper. When the box is fitting properly on the mat board, place the cover on the box. Set some hardcover books on top of the box, enough to weigh the box down to securely glue it, yet not too heavy to crush the box. Let dry overnight.

4. Follow the manufacturer's instructions to spray paint the inside and outside of the box and the cover green, using as many coats as necessary to achieve complete coverage. Spray in a well-ventilated area, preferably outside.

5. Select a variety of golfing pictures from the golf magazines, scorecards or photos. Use decorative edge scissors or simply tear the edges, leaving backgrounds around the pictures, or trim close to the object edges. Lay them out on the brim, sides and top of the box, referring to the photo for layout ideas. Make sure to have some pictures run off the edges; fold the pictures around the edges and glue onto the back or bottom side. You can also begin gluing with no layout in mind, and keep at it until you like the arrangement.

6. Put white craft glue on the paper plate until it is the size of a quarter. Add a few drops of water to thin it out, and mix well with the paintbrush. If you have a layout, remove all the pictures from the box and cover. Begin applying glue to the back of the bottom-most picture with the paintbrush. Place the picture on the box as shown in the Step 6 illustration, and smooth it out with your fingers or the brush to remove wrinkles. Keep layering on pictures until you are pleased with the design. Let dry.

7. Follow the manufacturer's instructions to apply 2 coats of spray finish. Paint the golf ball with white acrylic paint, or use a brand new ball. Hot-glue the ball to the center of the lid for a handle. Put an extra dab of glue just under the side of the ball facing the brim, and lay a tee in front of it. Hot-glue the second tee in place, making a criss-cross design in front of the golf ball handle.

Gone Fishing Wall Quilt

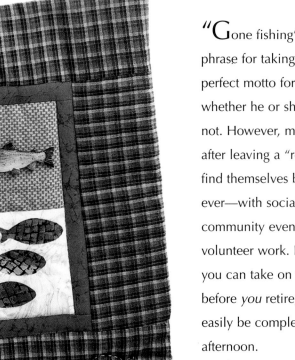

"Gone fishing" is the catch phrase for taking it easy, the perfect motto for every retiree whether he or she fishes or not. However, many people, after leaving a "real job," find themselves busier than ever—with social activities, community events and volunteer work. Rest assured, you can take on this quilt before *you* retire; it can easily be completed in one afternoon.

List of Materials

- 45" (115 cm) coordinating cotton fabrics: plaid, ¹/₂ yd. (0.5 m) for outer border and back; one light print; two dark prints, ¹/₈ yd. (0.15 m) each; 1¹/₂" (3.8 cm) square and eight 1¹/₄" x 5" (3.2 x 12.5 cm) assorted strips for the log cabin block
- Low-loft batting, ¹/₂ yd. (0.5 m)

- Fusible web
- Brass charms: fishhook, one; fish, two
- 3" (7.5 cm) flat resin fish
- Embroidery floss: dark brown; tan
- Embroidery needle
- ¹/₂" (1.3 cm) plastic rings, three

- ¹/₄" (6 mm) wooden dowel, 16" (40.5 cm)
- Pattern Page 173
- Miscellaneous items: scissors, ruler, tracing paper, pencil, transfer paper, straight pins, transparent nylon thread, matching sewing thread, sewing needle, iron, sewing machine, fabric glue

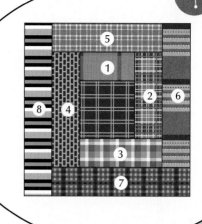

1. Wash and dry all fabrics without fabric softener; press. See the Step 1 illustration to make a log cabin square. Use the 1¹⁄₂″ (3.8 cm) square in the center and sew the 1¹⁄₄″ x 5″ (3.2 x 12.5 cm) strips in numerical order around it. Sew all fabrics right sides together using a ¹⁄₄″ (6 mm) seam allowance. Trim the ends of each strip even with the block and press the seams toward the darker color.

2. To make the 4-patch square, cut 1 dark and 2 light fabric squares the size of the finished log cabin square. Refer to the photo to sew the squares together.

3. For the inner border, cut one 1¹⁄₂″ x 45″ (3.8 x 115 cm) dark print strip. Sew the strip to each side of the quilt; trim the ends. Repeat to sew the strip to the top and bottom.

4. For the outer border, cut one 3¹⁄₂″ x 45″ (9 x 115 cm) strip. Repeat Step 3 to sew the strip to the sides, top and bottom of the quilt.

5. Trace the "Gone Fishing" pattern and transfer it to the top left square. Refer to Embroidery Stitches on page 159 to work backstitches for the words with 3 strands of dark brown floss.

6. Cut a square of batting and plaid fabric the same size as the quilt top. Layer batting; backing, face up; quilt top, face down. Sew the layers together leaving a 5″ (12.5 cm) opening. Trim the seams. Turn and slipstitch the opening closed.

7. To machine quilt, use thread to match the backing in the bobbin and transparent thread in the needle. Stitch-in-the-ditch around each block and border.

8. Follow the manufacturer's instructions to fuse the web to the back of the remaining dark fabric. Trace the fish pattern and cut out as indicated on the pattern. Refer to the photo to fuse 3 fish to the lower right square.

9. Trace the left and right fish patterns and transfer them to the upper left and lower right corners of the quilt border. Work running stitches around the fish and French knot air bubbles above the fish's mouth with 3 strands of tan floss.

10. Tack stitch the fish charms to the lower left corner of the inner border, and the hook to the center of the log cabin square. Glue the resin fish to the upper right square.

11. To hang the quilt, tack plastic rings evenly spaced across the top back and slide the dowel through the rings.

Rainbow Trout Clock

Any angler, especially if retired, will love to have a clock with this beautiful fish on it. Whenever glancing at the time, they'll be reminded of their favorite activity—for which they now have plenty of time.

List of materials

- Wooden upright bezel clock*, 2¹/₂" x 7" x 7¹/₂" (6.5 x 18 x 19.3 cm) with 4" (10 cm) round design area
- 14-count light seafoam Aida cloth, 5" (12.5 cm) square
- 6-strand skeins DMC embroidery floss in colors listed in Color Key

- No. 24 tapestry needle
- Miscellaneous items: scissors, ruler, iron, terrycloth towel, press cloth

*(See Sources on pg. 175 for purchasing information.)

1 Refer to the Cross-Stitch General Instructions and the Stitches on page 160 and the Stitch Chart to cross-stitch the design using 2 strands of cotton floss and 1 strand of rayon floss.

2 To backstitch the design, use 2 strands of ultra very dark turquoise (3808) to work the numerals and fish outline. Use 1 strand of ultra very dark turquoise (3808) for the fishing line and hook and 1 strand of bright orange-red (606) for the feathers on the fly.

3 Press the stitched design if necessary, and follow the manufacturer's instructions to mount the stitched design in the clock.

Rainbow Trout Clock Stitch Chart

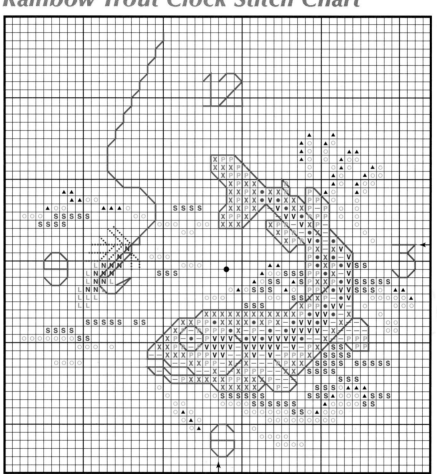

Rainbow Trout Clock Color Key

Symbol	DMC #	Color
N	606	Bright Orange-Red
S	826	Med. Blue
P	3348	Lt. Yellow Green
•	3808	Ultra Vy. Dk. Turquoise
X	3814	Dk. Aquamarine
−	30415	Pearl Gray
V	30603	Cranberry
L	30744	Pale Yellow
○	30800	Pale Delft
▲	35200	White
•••	606	Bright Orange-Red Backstitches
−	3808	Ultra Vy. Dk. Turquoise Backstitches

sweet sampler Pincushions

These sampler pincushions are a great retirement gift for someone who loves to sew. He or she will admire the clever sewing motif and the different stitches used in the ABC design. The pincushions will also be appreciated for their practicality.

List of Materials

- 14-count beige evenweave fabric, 8" (20.5 cm) squares, two
- 6-strand skeins of DMC embroidery floss in colors listed in Color Key

- No. 24 tapestry needle
- Scissors

- Polyester fiberfill
- Pattern Page 172

1 Refer to the Cross-Stitch General Instructions and Stitches on page 160, Embroidery Stitches on page 159, and the Stitch Charts on page 172 to cross-stitch each design using 2 strands of floss. Use 2 strands of ultra dark beaver gray (844) to work running stitch borders.

2 To stitch the ABC pincushion, backstitch using 2 strands of very dark terra cotta (3777) for lettering and grid pattern on yellow heart. Use ultra dark beaver gray (844) for remaining backstitches, 1 strand to outline hearts, 2 strands for stitch lines, and 2 strands for the cross-stitches above and below "ABC" and "123."

3 Use 2 strands of floss to work light navy blue (312) lazy daisy flowers with dark straw (3820) French knot centers and to work white French knots on red heart.

4 To stitch the sewing pincushion, use 2 strands of white to backstitch highlights on scissors handles and buttons. Use 2 strands of dark hunter green (3345) to backstitch thread lines on tomato pincushion. For blended shading stitches on the pincushion, use 1 strand of each color. Use ultra dark beaver gray (844) for remaining backstitches, 2 strands for pins and 1 strand for all other backstitches.

5 To finish each pincushion, align stitched front with backing fabric, wrong sides together. Using 2 strands of dark hunter green (3345) cross-stitch front to back over 2 fabric threads. Work every other stitch, making crosses on front and back, to achieve a finished look on each side and leave a small opening to stuff. Stuff with fiberfill and continue stitching to close. Trim fabric 10 threads beyond stitching line; pull threads to fringe.

Denim Blues Afghan

Although the crocheted white puff stitches are surrounded by two shades of blue, this afghan is guaranteed to chase the blues away. It will keep your favorite coworker cozy and warm when he or she relaxes to enjoy retirement—whether watching TV, reading a book or just taking a nap in the middle of the day.

List of Materials

- Worsted weight acrylic yarn, 3.5-oz. (99 g) skeins: white (A), six; light denim heather (B), denim heather (C), three each

- Size 10½/K aluminum crochet hook or size to obtain gauge

- Miscellaneous items: scissors; 3" x 6" (7.5 x 15 cm) cardboard piece

Gauge: 3 dc = 1″ (2.5 cm)
Size: Each strip = 4″ (10 cm) wide
Finished Afghan Size = Approximately 40″ x 60″ (102 x 152.5 cm)

Refer to the Crochet Abbreviations and Stitches on page 161.
Puff st: (Yo, insert hook in indicated st, yo and pull up a 3/4″ (2 cm) long lp) 3 times, yo and draw through 7 lps on hook.

To make each strip center (make 10), with white, ch 5; puff st in 4th ch from hook, dc in last ch; turn. (dc, puff st, dc).
Row 1: Ch 3 (counts as first dc), puff st in puff st, dc in top of beg ch-3; turn.
Rows 2-69: Rep Row 1. Fasten off.

Border:
Rnd 1 (right side): With right side facing, join light denim heather in beg ch at base of first puff st with sl st, ch 3 (counts as first dc), (dc, ch 2, 2 dc) in same ch; * working along sides of rows, work (dc, ch 1, 3 dc) in side of first dc, 2 dc in next dc, (3 dc in next dc, 2 dc in next dc) across to last dc, (3 dc, ch 1, dc) in last dc *, (2 dc, ch 2, 2 dc) in top of last puff st; rep bet *'s once; sl st in top of beg ch-3. Fasten off.
Rnd 2: With right side facing, join white at end of strip with sl st in ch-2 sp, ch 1, (sc, ch 3, sc) in same sp; * ch 3, sk next st, sc in next st, ch 3, sk next st, (sc, ch 3, sc) in next st, (ch 3, sk next st, sc in next st) across to next ch-1 sp at opposite end of strip, ch 3, (sc, ch 3, sc) in ch-1 sp, sk next st, sc in next st, ch 3, sk next st *, (sc, ch 3, sc) in end ch-2 sp; rep bet *'s once; sl st in beg sc. Fasten off.
Rnd 3: With right side facing, join denim heather at end of strip with sl st in ch-3 sp, ch 3 (counts as first dc), (dc, ch 2, 2 dc) in same sp; * 2 dc in each of next 2 sps, (dc, ch 1, dc) in next corner sp, 2 dc in each ch-3 sp across to next corner sp, (dc, ch 1, dc) in corner sp, 2 dc in each of next 2 sps *, (2 dc, ch 2, 2 dc) in end ch-3 sp; rep bet *'s once; sl st in top of beg ch-3. Fasten off.

To assemble the afghan, hold the strips right sides together and sew the long sides together with denim heather yarn, leaving the pointed ends free.

To make each tassel (make 20), wind 2 strands of white yarn lengthwise around the cardboard 20 times. Cut an 18″ (46 cm) length of yarn and insert 1 end under wrapped yarn at top of cardboard; see the Step 6A illustration. Pull tightly and tie securely. Remove yarn from cardboard. Wrap a second length of yarn tightly around tassel, 1¼″ (3.2 cm) from the top as shown in 6B. Trim tassel ends evenly. Attach a tassel at each point of the afghan.

6″

3″

1¼″

A

B

Springtime Mosaic Planter

Give a ray of sunshine for a retirement gift with this bright yellow and white mosaic planter. Not that the retiree isn't already sunny after leaving the "daily grind," but he or she can't help but smile seeing small pots of herbs, ivy or garden seedlings growing in this window box.

List of Materials

- 10¹/₂" x 6¹/₂" x 4³/₄" (26.8 x 16.3 x 12 cm) natural pine wood window box*
- Plaster kits with molds and microwaveable plaster*: fun shapes; bugs & critters
- Mixing bottle*
- Acrylic paints*: pastel plaster set; *indoor/outdoor gloss enamel:* yellow; white
- Gloss plaster glaze*
- Paintbrushes: small and medium flat; 1" (2.5 cm) sponge
- ³/₄" (2 cm) square mosaic ceramic tiles*: white; yellow; green

- Tile nippers*
- Mosaic tile adhesive*
- White tile grout*
- Tile sealer*
- Miscellaneous items: fine sandpaper, tack cloth, ¹/₂" (1.3 cm) masking tape, disposable palette, water basin, pencil, ruler, measuring tablespoon, plastic cup and spoon, paper towels, disposable gloves, soft cloth, safety goggles, newspapers, small disposable plastic container, craft stick, soft-bristle brush, household sponge, microwave oven (optional)

*(See Sources on pg. 175 for purchasing information.)

1 Sand the wood window box to smooth; wipe with a tack cloth. Basecoat the box with yellow and white gloss enamels; let dry between colors and steps. With yellow, paint the top beveled edge, ends of the box front and back, handle edges and the inside of the handles. Paint the box ends, and the back and inside of the box white.

2 Refer to the photo and the Step 2 illustration to use the masking tape to mask off and paint alternating white 1/2" (1.3 cm) square checks on the handles. The tile mosaic will cover the unpainted box front.

Unpainted box front—
tile will cover

3 Refer to the manufacturer's instructions to mix plaster, pour into molds and microwave to dry; unmold. Make a turtle, bunny, butterfly, snail and ladybug. Using the pastel plaster paints, refer to the photo to paint each critter. Apply 2 coats of gloss glaze.

4 To create the mosaic, refer to the photo to plan your design. Use tile adhesive to glue the pieces to the box front. Begin by gluing the plaster critters to the box. Then glue alternating green and white tiles in a rectangle around the edges, with the top horizontal row just below the yellow beveled edge. Leave a small space between tiles for the grout. Wearing safety goggles, use the tile nippers to cut tiles into small irregular shapes to fit around the plaster critters. Glue yellow tiles inside the green/white rectangle, using whole tiles where possible and filling in with partial tiles. Let dry thoroughly.

5 Follow the manufacturer's instructions to mix the grout with a craft stick in a small disposable container. Wearing gloves, press grout between the tiles, filling in all of the cracks. Be careful not to cover the plaster critters. Let set for 10-15 minutes.

6 Dampen the sponge to wipe off excess grout and smooth the edges. Rinse the sponge and repeat until just a haze of grout remains. When the grout is completely dry, rub off remaining grout residue with the soft-bristle brush. Use a soft cloth to buff the tile pieces to shine. To finish, apply 2 coats of tile sealer over the entire window box.

Garden Angel

Give your favorite retiree his or her own guardian angel—a garden angel! Cut the wood pieces, then paint them as an angel dressed in bib overalls. Topped with a straw hat, she extends a hand to feathered friends and carries a basket of garden bounty.

List of Materials

- Wood: pine; 2″ x 4″ x 43″ (5 x 10 x 109 cm); 1″ x 10″ x 12″ (2.5 x 25.5 x 30.5 cm); birch, 1/4″ x 14″ x 18″ (6 mm x 35.5 cm x 46 cm)
- 21/2″ (6.5 cm) wood ball, one
- 1/4″ (6 mm) wood dowel, one
- Tools: jigsaw; drill with 1/4″ and 1/8″ bits; hammer; 1″ (2.5 cm) nails
- 18-gauge hardware wire
- Acrylic paints: light ivory; slate blue; peach; persimmon; cayenne; black; empire gold; antique gold; midnight blue; Georgia clay; dark brown; leaf green; hunter green
- Paintbrushes: No. 20 flat; No. 1 liner; 1″ (2.5 cm) sponge; small stencil
- Buttons: 3/8″ (1 cm) white, four; 5/8″ (1.5 cm) brown, two
- 6″ (15 cm) straw hat, one
- Natural raffia
- Spanish moss
- Small basket, your choice, one

- 11/2″ to 2″ (3.8 to 5 cm) yellow silk flowers, eight
- Seed packets, five
- Glues: hot glue gun; wood
- Pattern Sheet
- Miscellaneous items: tracing and graphite paper, pencil, yardstick, stylus, scissors, wire cutters, fine sandpaper, tack cloth, disposable palette, brush basin, paper towels, masking tape

Trace the patterns onto tracing paper. Use graphite paper and a stylus to transfer the outlines only onto the wood pieces indicated on the patterns and mark the drill holes. Use the Body Top Painting Pattern to draw the angled shoulder lines and mark the drill hole at 1 end of the 2x4. Refer to the Body Guide for the bottom point at the opposite end. Cut the wood pieces and drill the holes as indicated. Using the 1/4" bit, also drill a 3/4" (2 cm) deep hole in the center bottom of the wood ball. Sand rough edges smooth and wipe with a tack cloth.

Refer to the Painting Instructions and Techniques on page 156. Paint the front, back and edges of wood pieces, letting dry between paint colors and each step. Use the sponge brush to basecoat the sign and wings ivory. Float slate blue to shade the edges. Transfer the message to the sign. Use the liner brush and slate blue to paint the message, dotting the letter ends with the stylus. Use the sponge brush to paint the crows black. Use the liner brush to dot the eyes with antique gold.

Garden Angel Body Guide

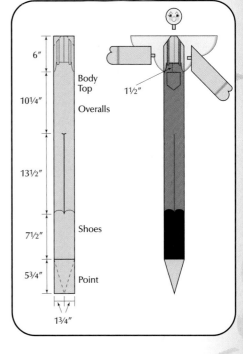

Use the sponge brush to paint the wood ball peach. With the drill hole at center bottom, transfer the face painting pattern to the front. Float persimmon to shade the cheeks, then cayenne to shade the nose. Dot the eyes black with a dowel. Use the liner brush and black to paint the eyebrows, eyelashes, smile lines and mouth. Paint ivory comma stroke highlights on eyes, cheeks and nose.

Transfer the Body Top Painting Pattern Lines to the 2x4. Refer to the Body Guide to draw the painting lines for the shoes. Use the sponge and flat brushes to basecoat as follows: the shoes, black; the overalls and the separate pocket piece, slate blue; and the shirt, antique gold. Transfer the sleeve lines to the arms. Paint the hands peach and the sleeves empire gold. Float antique gold to shade the bottom of each sleeve.

Float antique gold to shade the bottom shirt edges and center front opening. Float midnight blue to shade the edges of the overall straps, bib and pocket. Refer to the Body Guide to draw a 13 1/2" (34.3 cm) crotch line; float midnight blue to shade. With the liner brush and Georgia clay, paint topstitching lines around the pocket and upper bib.

To paint the basket, thin brown paint with water; use the stencil brush to stipple soil around the basket bottom. Paint the carrots with the liner brush and Georgia clay. Use the stencil brush to stipple hunter green grass and leaf green carrot tops.

Assemble the angel referring to the Body Guide. Use wood glue to glue the pocket to the overalls 1 1/2" (3.8 cm) below the bib center top. From the wood dowel, cut three 1 1/2" (3.8 cm) lengths. Glue 1 length in the hole in the head and each arm. Let dry, then glue the opposite end of each dowel to attach the head to the body and the arms (thumbs up) on opposite sides. Nail the wings to the angel. Cut two 18" (46 cm) lengths of wire. Wire the sign to the right arm through the bottom drill holes; twist the ends together at front and wrap around a pencil to curl. Cut one 3" (7.5 cm) and one 5" (12.5 cm) wire. Glue a wire in the drill hole at the bottom of each crow; glue the opposite ends in the top of the right arm with crows facing each other.

Glue a brown button to the bottom of each overall strap and white buttons down the shirt center front. Hot-glue Spanish moss to the head for hair, on the right arm for a nest and inside the basket. Glue the hat angled back on the head. Arrange and glue the seed packets and flowers inside the basket. Insert several strands of raffia through the drill hole in the left hand, then tie in a large bow around the basket handle. Tie a raffia bow around the angel's neck.

Birthdays

Here you'll find some of the best ways to say "Best Wishes" to each unique person in your life. Armed with these fresh ideas, you're ready for a full year of birthdays for children, parents, grandparents, coworkers and friends.

CELEBRATE

March

MOM

Happy Birthday Angels

More precious than the jewels themselves, these adorable wood angels painted with birthstone colors are sure to be treasured and loved. Each is complete with a head full of curls and laced-up shoes and carries a special gift or decoration to the angel birthday party.

List of Materials

For Each Angel

- Wood: doll form (candle cup and large wood bead may be used); 1/2" x 5/8" (1.3 x 1.5 cm) wood spools, two; 14 mm wood beads, red, two; 1 1/8" x 1 5/8" x 7/16" (2.8 x 4 x 1.2 cm) wood base

- Wire paper twist, 5 1/4" (13.2 cm)

- 140-pound (63 kg) watercolor paper, 4" (10 cm) square

- Medium natural string doll hair

- Fine-line black permanent marker

- Acrylic paints: apricot (all); baroque pearl (June); crimson (all, July); sky blue (April); light yellow green (March, August); marina blue (March); red (January); turquoise (December); pink (October); blue (September); purple (February); white (all); green (May); yellow ochre (November)

- Paintbrushes: Nos. 4 and 10 flat; fine spotter; small round fabric

- 1/2" x 42" (1.3 x 107 cm) muslin

- Heavy white crochet thread

- Glues: white craft; low-temp glue gun

For Assorted Trims

- Purchased miniatures: 3/4" (2 cm) gold novelty ring; gifts; teddy bear; ribbon roses; basket

- 3" x 5" (7.5 x 12.5 cm) cardstock, your color choice, two

- 5/8" (1.5 cm) green ribbon bow

- Green tissue paper, 2" (5 cm) square

- Seed beads, any color, two

- 22-gauge brass wire

- Pattern Page 173

- Miscellaneous items: scissors, tracing and transfer paper, pencil, stylus, disposable palette, container for water, craft knife, wire cutters, old magazine, round toothpicks, bottle cap; 1" (2.5 cm) flat button, sponge, thin bamboo skewer or stick

1 Hot-glue wood spool legs to wide end of doll form. Bend a 1/4" (6 mm) loop on each wire paper twist end for hands; paint apricot stone. Spiral-wrap muslin strip around paper twist to make arms; spot-glue to secure. Wrap middle of wire sparingly where arms will be glued to angel back.

2 Refer to Painting Instructions and Techniques on page 156. Paint doll head with apricot and the wood bead shoes with crimson. Lightly blush cheeks with an apricot/crimson mix. Paint body, arms, legs and wood base with color indicated in the Materials List. For March, paint with a yellow green/marina blue mix. For June, basecoat with white, then baroque pearl.

3 Trace patterns and transfer face pattern. Draw details with fine-line black marker as seen in the Step 3 illustration. Cut out wings. Lightly sponge-paint front and back with body color. Untwist 2" (5 cm) of string hair; do not cut off. Apply hot glue to top, sides and back of head. Arrange hair on glue; trim. Glue halo to head.

4 Glue center of arms, then wings to back. Refer to the photo to shape arms. Hot-glue red bead shoes to legs, then shoes to wood base. Paint a white "X" on each shoe for shoestrings. Dot ends of "X" with white. Tie 2 small crochet cotton bows. Glue a bow to each shoe above the "X." Use a fine-line black marker to print month on front of wood base.

5 Glue a purchased miniature in angel hands or make 1 of the following trims and glue to hands:

Cake: Glue bottle cap "cake" to a button "platter." Cover cake with swirls of hot glue. Cut off three 1/4" (6 mm) round toothpick ends and push into glue for candles. Paint cake white, candles blue and candle tips crimson.

Star Bouquet: Cut out stars. Paint front and back of each star with desired color. Cut five 2" to 31/2" (5 to 9 cm) lengths of wire. Twist ends together. Glue a star to each wire.

Kite or Banner: Cut from cardstock and print desired message. Wrap and glue end of banner around a 31/2" (9 cm) length of bamboo skewer and insert into hands as shown in the Step 5 illustration. Glue an 8" (20.5 cm) length of wire between kite pieces for string. Push wire end through angel hand and twist around pencil to curl.

Rose Basket or Bouquet: Twist 3 rose stems together. For bouquet, trim stems to 1/2" (1.3 cm) and wrap in green tissue paper. For basket, trim to 3/8" (1 cm); glue in basket. Glue bow to basket front.

Greeting Card: Fold a 7/8" x 11/2" (2.2 x 3.8 cm) piece of cardstock in half. Paint a red heart on center front. Print "FOR YOU" above and below heart.

Pinwheel: Cut two 11/2" (3.8 cm) squares of solid contrasting colors from a magazine picture. Glue squares wrong sides together. Transfer pattern to square and cut out. Bend each tab to the center matching dots; spot glue. Glue a seed bead to pinwheel center and a toothpick to the back.

Bear Birthday Bash

Baby food and jelly jars filled with gum balls replace tummies on readymade bears for a birthday jamboree. Cut an inexpensive plush bear apart, then glue teddy's head and paws to a jar with yummies inside. The large bear closely guards the giant foam lollipops on the colorful centerpiece. Create a smaller version as a perfect favor for every young party-goer to take home!

List of Materials

- Clear glass jars washed and dried: $2^{1}/_{2}$" x 4" (6.5 x 10 cm) jelly or pickle; 2" x $2^{3}/_{4}$" (5 x 7 cm) baby food, one for each flavor

- Plush stuffed bears: 12" (30.5 cm), one; 8" (20.5 cm), one for each favor

- 45" (115 cm) bright print fabric, $^{1}/_{2}$ yd. (0.5 m)

- Double-sided sheet adhesive

- Assorted trims, to coordinate

- with fabric: chenille stems; $^{1}/_{8}$" to $^{3}/_{8}$" (3 mm to 1 cm) satin ribbons; curling ribbon, five colors; $^{1}/_{2}$" (1.3 cm) pom poms, one for each bear

- Gum balls, multi-color, or other candy to fill jars

- 36" (91.5 cm) wood dowels: $^{1}/_{8}$" (3 mm), one; $^{3}/_{8}$" (1 cm), two

- Watercolor paper or canvas, 2" x 3" (5 x 7.5 cm) for each favor

- $3^{1}/_{2}$" (9 cm) mylar balloon

- 1" (2.5 cm) Styrofoam® discs, 4" (10 cm), four; 8" (20.5 cm), two

- Cellophane: green, blue, hot pink, yellow

- Hot glue gun

- Pattern Sheet

- Miscellaneous items: scissors, ruler, pinking shears, floral wire, wire cutters, sewing needle and matching thread, fine-point black permanent marker

1 To make each jar bear, carefully remove head, arms and legs from each plush bear. It may be necessary to cut fabric around the discs that hold the bears together. If so, glue opening closed.

2 For each collar, use pinking shears to cut a 2" x 16" (5 x 40.5 cm) fabric strip for a large bear and a 1 1/2" x 16" (3.8 x 40.5 cm) for a small bear. Sew a gathering stitch along 1 long strip edge and pull threads to form a circle. Glue ends of strip together.

3 To assemble, center and glue collar on jar lid, then glue head on collar. Fill each jar with gum balls. Screw lid on jar, then refer to the photo and the Step 3 illustration to glue arms and legs on jar sides. Tie ribbon bows and glue under bear's chin above collar.

4 To make the bear's hat, refer to the manufacturer's instructions to adhere sheet adhesive to fabric back. Trace the patterns as directed and cut from adhesive-backed fabric. Remove backing from hat as indicated on the pattern, and form fabric into a cone shape. Glue a pom pom to hat tip and a chenille stem around bottom hat edge. Glue hat to bear's head.

5 To make favors, see the Step 5 illustration to cut a triangle shape from watercolor paper to make each pennant. Write name on pennant. Cut a 3" (7.5 cm) length of 1/8" (3 mm) dowel. Glue pennant to dowel, and dowel to bear's paw.

6 To make the centerpiece, glue balloon to bear's paw. Cut 3/8" (1 cm) dowels as follows: 10" (25.5 cm); 12" (30.5 cm); 13" (33 cm); 15" (38 cm). Insert dowel end into edge of a 4" (10 cm) foam disc for each lollipop. Cut a 16" (40.5 cm) square of each color of cellophane and a 1/2" x 16" (1.3 x 40.5 cm) pinked fabric strip. Wrap foam disc with cellophane, gather at base and tie with fabric strip.

7 For the base, stack and glue 8" (20.5 cm) foam discs together. Cut an 8" (20.5 cm) fabric circle and glue to top of base. Use pinking shears to cut a 2 1/4" x 45" (6 x 115 cm) fabric strip. Sew gathering stitches on long fabric edge and pull threads to gather. Spot glue gathered strip around base sides.

8 Refer to the photo to insert lollipops into base behind bear, poking holes in fabric with scissors before inserting dowels. Cut long strands of curling ribbon. Align strands and loosely loop 3 or 4 times. Tie ribbon loops together with a short strand. Refer to the photo and use floral wire to attach loops to base. Set large bear on base.

Salt Shaker Angels

A snippet of this and a pinch of that transforms plain salt and pepper shakers or spice bottles into wonderful little birthday angels in just minutes! Fill the bottle with colorful potpourri or bath salts, decorate with bits of crafting leftovers and they're ready to deliver tiny birthday blessings to your family and friends. Dressed in simple country trims, they sprinkle charm wherever they go.

List of Materials

- Clear glass salt shaker or other small glass bottle with lid
- Potpourri or bath salts, your choice, enough to fill bottle
- 1¼" (3.2 cm) wooden ball
- Peach acrylic paint
- ½" to 1" (1.3 to 2.5 cm) lace, ½ yd. (0.5 m)

- Quilted fabric scrap, 4" (10 cm) square
- Spanish moss
- Assorted trims: satin ribbon, gold cord, ribbon rose, gold star garland (optional)
- Miscellaneous items: scissors, paintbrush, hot glue gun, small piece of white paper, fine-line black marker

1. To make each angel, wash and dry the glass bottle thoroughly. Fill the bottle with potpourri or bath salts. Trace the pattern to tracing paper and cut out. Adjust the size of the heart wings to correspond with the bottle.

2. Paint the wooden ball with peach paint. Let dry. Glue the ball to the neck of the bottle.

3. Depending on the width of the lace, glue 1 or 2 rows of lace around the neck. Tie a small ribbon bow and glue over the lace below the chin, as shown in the Step 3 illustration. Tie a small bow with gold cord and glue over the ribbon bow. Glue the ribbon rose to the center of the bow.

4. For the hair, glue Spanish moss to the top, back and sides of the wooden ball head.

5. For the halo, glue the shaker lid to the top of the head. If desired, substitute a loop of gold cord or star garland, such as shown on the middle angel.

6. To finish, glue the heart wings to the back of the angel. If desired, use a marker to write a message on a small rectangle of white paper and glue it to the front of the angel.

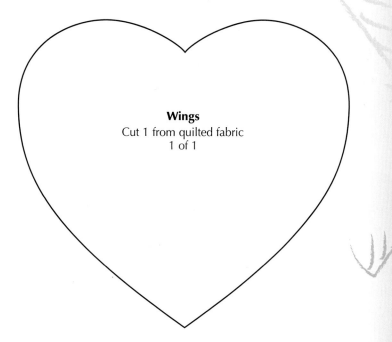

Wings
Cut 1 from quilted fabric
1 of 1

Fluffy Lamb Puppet

This fleecy pal will be a sure hit with a little one for a birthday gift. The puppet will fire up every child's imagination and will be loved and snuggled in every spare moment.

List of Materials

- 45" (115 cm) fabrics: white polyester lamb's wool such as shearling fleece or Berber, 1/4 yd. (0.25 m); velour: white; pink, 1/8 yd. (0.15 m) each; pink polyester satin, 1/8 yd. (0.15 m)
- 1/4" (6 mm) pink satin ribbon, 1/4 yd. (0.25 m)
- 3/8" (1 cm) jingle bell, one
- Polyester fiberfill

- Pink embroidery floss
- Black carpet thread
- Pattern Sheet
- Miscellaneous items: scissors, tracing paper, pencil, ruler, straight pins, matching sewing thread, embroidery and sewing needles, air-soluble marker, sewing machine

Stitch up and in the
following order:
1, 2, 3, 1;
4, 3;
5, 6, 3, 6;
7, 8, 6, 8;
9, 10, 8, 10

10   8   6   3   1
  9   2
      7   5   4

I Trace the patterns from the pattern section and cut from appropriate fabrics. Mark all dots with an air-soluble marker. Sew all fabrics right sides together using a 1/4" (6 mm) seam allowance, unless otherwise indicated. Refer to the Embroidery Stitches on page 159.

2 On 1 face piece, see the Step 2 illustration and use black carpet thread to work straight stitches for the eyelashes. Use 6 strands of pink embroidery floss to embroider the mouth and nostrils. Work French knots for the nostrils, and a long straight stitch between the 2 mouth dots for the mouth. With wrong sides together, sew the 2 face pieces together, leaving them open between the top dots. Stuff lightly and slipstitch the opening closed.

3 Pin the face to the head. Stitch between dots; clip, then stitch from dots to sides.

4 Pin and sew 1 pink and 1 white ear together, leaving the bottom open. Clip at the tip; turn right side out. Repeat for the second ear. With the pink fabric to the inside, fold each ear in half and sew across the raw edge. Matching raw edges, pin ears to head between dots. Sew the ears to the right side of the head.

5 See the Step 5A illustration to sew the upper half of mouth piece to the back of the face piece along the previous stitching, matching the dots. Flip the other side of the mouth piece down and pin it to the neck piece. See the Step 5B illustration to sew lower half of mouth to chin area of neck piece between the dots.

5

Stitch upper
half of mouth
to back of face
along previous
stitching

A

Stitch lower
half of mouth
to chin area of
neck piece

B

6 To finish the puppet, pin 1 puppet body piece to the head piece, overlapping head piece and matching dotted line. The ends will not meet. Sew across the dotted line. Finger press the seam open and flip the body piece over. See the Step 6 illustration to pin and sew body to head, turn over, and sew bottom of head to body. Stuff lightly from the sides, between the 2 stitching lines.

7 Sew the second puppet body to the straight edge of the neck piece. Pushing the ears to the inside, pin and sew the side seams together. Turn under and sew a 1/2" (1.3 cm) hem on the lower edge.

8 Make a bow with the pink ribbon. Sew the jingle bell to the center of the bow, then sew the bow to the top of the lamb's head.

Head →   Face

Stitch body to
head, turn
over, and sew
bottom of
head to body

Body

6

Play Table for Tots

Imagine the hours of pleasant play a child will have sitting at this colorful table with its matching stool. This is a birthday gift sure to please the child and his or her parents. Easy to apply graphic tapes create bright borders that are filled in with round and star stickers. The surface is then protected with a waterproof resin. Any spills or "creative" messes are simply wiped away.

List of Materials

- Unfinished wood: 20" (51 cm) round unfinished table with 3 straight screw-on legs; 13³/4" (35 cm) tapered legs with screws, 3, to replace table legs; 8" (20.5 cm) round plaque with beveled edge, for the stool
- Gloss graphic tapes: ¹/32" (0.75 mm) red and blue; ¹/16" (1.5 mm) white, red, blue and yellow; ¹/8" (3 mm) red—check in an art supply store
- ¹/4" (6 mm) round and star stickers: red; blue; orange; pink; yellow; purple; green
- Wood sealer/primer
- White, nonyellowing, spray paint
- Gloss acrylic enamel paints: red; green; blue; yellow
- Transparent brush-on sealant
- Pint kit of clear waterproof epoxy resin
- Sponge paintbrushes: 1" (2.5 cm); 2" (5 cm)
- Leg hardware for stool
- White plastic furniture leg caps, 3
- Tools: screwdriver; drill; saw
- Pattern Page 174
- Miscellaneous items: pencil, fine sandpaper, tack cloth, tracing paper, graphite paper, stylus, carpenter's square, yardstick, scissors, paper towels, plastic drop cloth, petroleum jelly, putty knife

1 To make the table, unscrew legs and set aside. Sand table top and purchased tapered legs to smooth. Wipe with tack cloth. Apply coat of sealer/primer. Spray top with several coats of white paint. Let dry. Paint outer edge red. Paint 1 leg each with 2 or more coats of red, yellow and blue.

2 Use yardstick to find center of top and lightly mark with pencil. Use the carpenter's square to draw a 3" (7.5 cm) square in center. Trace the center circle in the Graphic Tape Placement Guide on page 174. Transfer to center top of table with graphite paper and stylus. Paint circle yellow. Paint square with 2 or more coats of red, as shown in the Step 2 illustration.

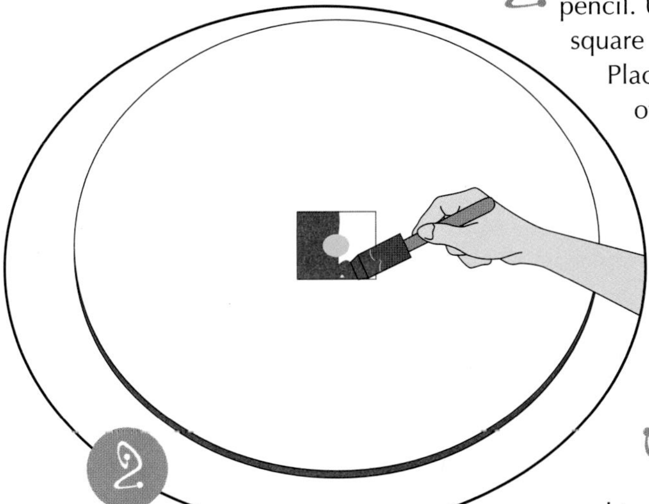

3 Refer to the Placement Guide to position tapes around center square, extending lines to edge. To fill in the design with stickers, start at center. Adhere a star, then 2 circles and repeat to fill each row.

4 Apply 2 or more coats of transparent brush-on sealant on top only. Let dry. Adhere 1/16" (1.5 mm) red tape around upper edge of top. Apply 2 coats of sealant to entire edge.

5 Before applying resin, read the epoxy resin manufacturer's instructions carefully. Turn top over and liberally coat the underside edge with petroleum jelly. Cover level work surface with drop cloth. Place a box or other level object, smaller than table top, on drop cloth. Place table top, right side up, on box.

6 Mix resin and pour slowly from the center of top outward. Resin will spread slightly after pouring. Every 15 to 20 minutes (for the first hour), use putty knife to scrape off any resin that drips over edge. Let dry for 24 hours. Wipe off petroleum jelly and scrape off any stray drips from underside edge. Screw in legs.

7 To make the stool, cut the legs from the table to 8" (20.5 cm). Sand the plaque and legs until smooth. Wipe with tack cloth. Coat with wood primer.

8 Spray plaque top with several coats of white. Paint edge red. Paint 1 leg each blue, yellow and green applying 2 or more coats.

9 See the Step 9 illustration to apply tapes to the beveled edge of top. Refer to the photo to apply stickers around top edge.

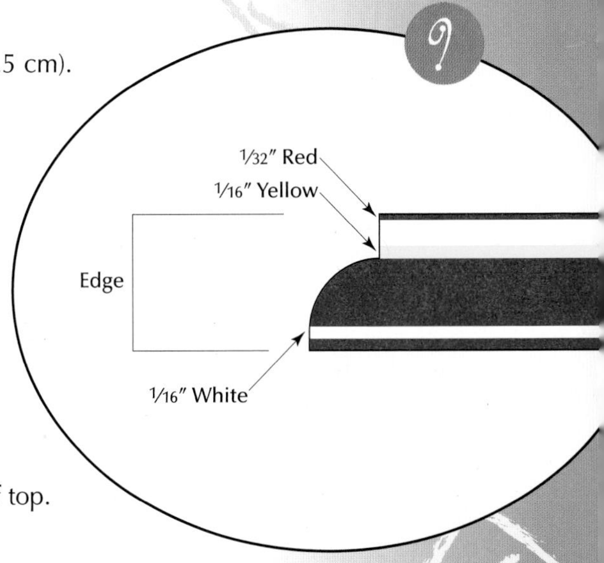

10 To finish, coat top and legs with 2 or 3 coats of sealant. Let dry. Attach leg hardware to underside of top. Screw in legs. Push plastic caps over leg ends.

1/32" Red
1/16" Yellow
Edge
1/16" White

Leapin' Larry, the Friendly Frog

Birthday kids will leap at the chance to frolic with this friendly fellow, who is sporting a green gingham body and a cotton batting tummy. He's willing to leave his comfy lily pad in exchange for lots of hugs to his squeezable body. His button joints let him pose and keep his legs firmly planted on the ground even when he's being hugged.

List of materials

- 45" (115 cm) cotton fabrics: green mini-check, ¼ yd. (0.25 m); ½" x 8" (1.3 x 20.5 cm) strip for hatband, your choice
- Natural cotton batting, 6" x 9" (15 x 23 cm)
- Polyester fiberfill
- 4-hole flat buttons: 1" (2.5 cm) white, two; dark green: ½" (1.3 cm), four; ¾" (2 cm), two
- Needles: sewing; soft-sculpture

- 4" (10 cm) straw hat
- Polypropylene mini pellets, ¾ cup (75 mL)
- Hot glue gun (optional)
- Pattern Sheet
- Miscellaneous items: tracing paper, pencil, scissors, pinking shears, sewing machine and matching thread, colored chalk, stuffing tool, ruler

1 Trace the patterns and cut out as indicated; use pinking shears to cut legs outside traced line. Transfer pattern markings with chalk. Sew fabrics right sides together using a 3/8" (1 cm) seam allowance unless otherwise indicated. Trim seams and clip curves as necessary.

2 Sew body pieces together between A and B dots, sewing around top of head and back. Sew tummy gusset to each body piece between A and B dots, leaving a small opening at bottom. Turn and firmly stuff; pour pellets in last to weight bottom. Slipstitch opening.

3 Pair and sew legs, wrong sides together, stuffing as you sew. Machine needle should be secured in fabric when stuffing to keep stitching line straight.

4 To sew back legs to the body, thread the soft-sculpture needle with doubled thread. Refer to the pattern to tack a 3/4" (2 cm) green button on 1 leg, inserting needle through body and opposite leg; slide on matching button on other leg. Repeat 3 times and knot thread; see the Step 4 illustration.

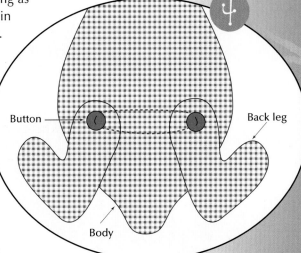

Button

Back leg

Body

5 Refer to the pattern to sew front legs on each side of upper gusset in the same way as the back legs were done in Step 4, tacking a 1/2" (1.3 cm) green button at the same time.

6 Follow Step 4 to sew eyes to head, stacking 1/2" (1.3 cm) green button pupils on 1" (2.5 cm) white button eyes. Pull thread taut to form shallow indentations.

7 Tie the 8" (20.5 cm) fabric strip around hat crown. Place or glue hat on frog head.

Floral Treasure Box

Paint an array of colorful blossoms to bring this wonderful wooden cabinet to life. It's a perfect birthday gift for storing favorite baubles and beads, or use it to brighten the kitchen where it can hold teas and other treats. Give it empty or stash it full of goodies—the choice is yours!

List of Materials

- 5" x 10¼" x 13¾" (12.5 x 26 x 35 cm) four-drawer wooden cabinet*
- Acrylic paints: buttercream; French blue; bright pink; ivory white; bayberry; violet pansy; sunflower
- Paintbrushes: No. 1 script liner; Nos. 1 and 3 round; Nos. 4 and 8 shader; 1" (2.5 cm) sponge
- ½" (1.3 cm) painters masking tape

- Matte acrylic spray finish
- Pattern Page 174
- Miscellaneous items: fine sandpaper, tack cloth, tracing paper, graphite paper, pencil, kneaded eraser, stylus, ruler, disposable palette, water basin, paper towels

*(See Sources on pg. 175 for purchasing information.)

1 Refer to the Painting Instructions and Techniques on page 156. Basecoat the entire cabinet with buttercream. Let dry between coats, colors and steps. Sand lightly to smooth and wipe with the tack cloth. Apply a second coat of buttercream.

2 Refer to the photo for paint placement. Paint the cabinet top and 1 drawer front bayberry, and the base and 1 drawer French blue; leave 2 drawers, drawer pulls and the balls on the base buttercream.

3 Make a lattice background on 1 buttercream drawer by applying tape in evenly spaced diagonal strips. Paint the open spaces with ivory white, let dry and remove the tape. Repeat the process, applying the tape in the opposite direction.

4 Divide 1 buttercream drawer into 8 equal vertical stripes. Tape off and paint stripes, alternating bayberry and French blue between buttermilk.

5 Trace the patterns to tracing paper; refer to the photo for placement. Use the ruler and pencil to draw diagonal placement lines for the daisy and pansy designs; see the Step 5 illustration. Use the graphite paper and stylus to transfer a rose design to the lattice drawer, a daisy design to the French blue drawer, a tulip to each buttercream stripe and a pansy design to the bayberry drawer. Erase placement lines.

6 To paint the roses, mix ivory white and bright pink to make soft pink. Shade around the petals with bright pink and highlight with various shades of bright pink and ivory white mixes. Paint stems and leaves bayberry; extend stems with the liner as desired.

7 To paint the daisies, use a round brush and ivory white to paint 1-stroke petals. Dot each daisy center with sunflower paint.

8 To paint the tulips, paint the petals bright pink and highlight each petal and the flower bottom edge with a light pink mix of bright pink and ivory white. Paint stems and leaves bayberry.

9 To paint the pansies, paint the petals violet pansy and each inner section buttercream. Mix violet pansy and ivory white to make light purple to highlight between and around the petal edges. Use the liner brush and violet pansy to paint petal crease lines around the outer edge of the buttercream inner section. Add a buttermilk highlight on 1 side of the pansy. Dot each center with sunflower paint.

10 For each drawer pull, paint a violet pansy and bright pink diagonal stripe across the top. Paint opposite diagonal stripes using bayberry and French blue. Spray with acrylic finish.

Fabulous Floral Soaps

You can give the hottest item at the next birthday get-together with your gal pals with these little heart-shaped soaps. Pour the lemon-scented soap mixture directly over silk or dried flower blossoms to suspend them inside the bar when the soap hardens. As pretty as can be, they're priced around $6 each at bath shops, but you can make them for as little as 50¢—desirable handmade gifts that won't break your budget. Better yet, you can mix 'n' mold them in no time at all!

List of Materials

- Unscented glycerin soap*, 4-oz. (113 g) bar
- 2-oz. (57 g) heart soap molds*, 2
- Yellow food coloring, 3 drops
- Lemon fragrance oil*, 20 drops

- Assorted small silk or dried flowers and leaves, your choice
- Miscellaneous items: mixing spoon, small saucepan, stove, plastic wrap, small scissors, wire cutters

*(See Sources on pg. 175 for purchasing information.)

1 Melt the glycerin soap in a saucepan over low heat, stirring constantly until liquefied. Remove from heat and stir in food coloring and fragrance oil until well blended. Spoon a thin layer of soap mixture into the heart molds.

2 Cut the stems from the flower blossoms and leaves, trimming the silks to smooth any ragged edges. Refer to the photo and the Step 2 illustration to arrange a few blossoms with some greenery in each soap, removing the flower calyxes if necessary. Pour the remaining soap mixture into the molds. Let set for 3 hours or until hard.

3 Remove the soaps from the molds and wrap individually in plastic wrap.

Paper Patch Lapel Pins

Create a one-of-a-kind pin for a one-of-a-kind friend on her birthday. Begin with corrugated cardboard, then simply tear watercolor paper, painted with washes of color, into small pieces to create the design. Add a tiny raffia bow and small brass charms to finish with flair. Each one is sure to be special and unique, reflecting the hobbies or loves of each of your friends.

List of Materials

For 5 Pins

- Corrugated kraft cardboard, 6" (15 cm) square
- Watercolor paper, 9" x 12" (23 x 30.5 cm) sheet
- Acrylic paints: blue; green; burgundy; brown

- Brass charms: girl, two; trowel, two; watering can; potted tulip; scissors; key; rake, one each
- Decorative-edge scissors: scallop; pinking
- Natural raffia

- 1" (2.5 cm) pin backs, five
- Glues: white craft; hot glue gun
- Miscellaneous items: pencil, ruler, scissors, water container, small paintbrush, disposable palette, fine-point black permanent marker

1 Measure and cut 1 each of the following pieces of corrugated cardboard using your choice of scissors: 1³/4″ x 2¹/4″ (4.5 x 6 cm); 1¹/2″ x 2¹/8″ (3.8 x 5.3 cm); 2¹/2″ x 1¹/4″ (6.5 x 3.2 cm); 2¹/2″ x 1¹/2″ (6.5 x 3.8 cm); 2″ (5 cm) square.

2 Cut the watercolor paper into 4 pieces. Brush water onto the paper to dampen. Put a drop of each paint color on a separate section of the palette. Thin each color with water until transparent. Brush a different color of paint on each piece of paper. Let dry.

3 Refer to the photo to tear or cut the watercolor paper into small, irregular shaped pieces. Tear a small heart from the green paper.

4 Refer to the photo and the Step 4 illustration to arrange and glue the paper shapes and charms on the front of each pin. Use craft glue for the paper and hot glue for the charms.

5 Tie 5 small raffia bows and glue 1 to each pin. Write "friends" on the pin with the 2 girl charms. Hot-glue a pin back to each pin.

Stenciled Foam Coasters

Add a bright touch to a birthday with colorful craft foam coasters. Besides being easy and economical, these foam coasters are such fun to make. Just cut the foam for the coasters and stencil with cute cup designs. Then quick-stitch shapes to make the holder. Even the kids can help!

List of Materials

- Craft foam: lime; yellow; pink; royal; orange; purple, one sheet each
- Cup stencils of your choice
- Stencil paints: light blue; blue; yellow; yellow green; green
- Stencil brush, one for each color
- Black embroidery floss
- Fine-line black permanent marking pen
- Miscellaneous items: ruler, pinking shears, scissors, masking tape, paper towels, embroidery needle

1 To make the coasters, use the pinking shears to cut two 4″ (10 cm) squares from each color craft foam.

2 To stencil, use a paper towel to remove the protective film from the surface of the stencil paint. Use a new stencil brush for each color family. Fill the stencil brush with color and wipe the excess on a paper towel. Always begin on the stencil itself and work into the open areas. Apply color in a dabbing or circular motion holding the brush in a perpendicular position. Use masking tape to hold the stencil in place and block off open areas not presently being stenciled. Let stencil paint dry for several hours.

3 To stencil each coaster, position a cup design centered on desired color coaster. Stencil the various parts of the cup design using a combination of the stencil paint colors as desired, as shown in the Step 3 illustration. Repeat to make 12 coasters.

4 Use the black marker to outline the cups with broken lines. Draw wavy lines and dots around the coaster edges.

5 To make the holder, use the pinking shears to cut 1 purple and 2 pink 2¼″ x 4¾″ (6 x 12 cm) foam rectangles. Also cut two 2¼″ (6 cm) yellow foam squares.

6 Use the marking pen to draw wavy lines and dots around the edges of the pink and yellow foam shapes. Use the pink rectangles for the sides, the yellow squares for the ends and the purple rectangle for the bottom. Refer to the photo to match edges and use the embroidery floss to whipstitch them together. Also whip-stitch around the top edges. Place the coasters in the holder.

Mom & Dad Gift Cups

These perky hand-painted cups are a treat in themselves for Mom and Dad. But wait until they see the goodies you've stashed inside! The roomy size of latté cups makes them perfect for gift baskets of (what else?) gourmet coffees, crunchy biscuits, aromatic teas or luscious cocoas. Wrap with tissue paper as shown, or use clear cellophane or tulle to leave nothing to the imagination.

List of Materials

For Each Cup

- 22-oz. (700 mL) white ceramic latté cup

- Stencil cleaner

- Air-dry enamel paints: gloss black; *for the Mom cup only:* lavender; rose mauve; baby blue; *for the Dad cup only:* country blue; yellow green; Christmas green

- Paintbrushes: No. 3 soft round; liner

- Pattern Sheet

- Miscellaneous items: vinegar, paper towels, tracing paper, graphite paper, pencil, disposable palette, small plastic container, toothpicks (optional)

1 To paint each cup, wash with warm soapy water, then rinse and dry thoroughly. The paints are nontoxic but are not recommended for use on surfaces with direct food contact. To prepare the area to be painted, position the handle on the appropriate right or left side and wipe the center front of the cup with a paper towel dipped in vinegar. Do not touch this area with your hands as you paint.

2 Trace the appropriate pattern to tracing paper. Lightly transfer the pattern to the prepared painting area on the cup with graphite paper and pencil. Refer to the Painting Instructions and Techniques on page 156. Follow the enamel paint manufacturer's instructions. Deco-Art™ air-dry enamels recommend the use of a dry brush. Do not thin the paints with water. Let dry between paint colors and steps.

3 To paint the Mom cup, basecoat the letters "M" lavender and the center heart rose mauve. Use the brush end in lavender to paint small dots 1/8" (3 mm) apart on the heart.

4 To paint flowers on the letters "M," paint rose mauve medium dots 3/8" (1 cm) apart for the flower centers. Then paint 6 baby blue small dot petals around each flower center.

5 Refer to the pattern and use the liner brush and black to paint short stitch lines around the heart and letters.

6 To paint the Dad cup, basecoat the letters "D" country blue and the letter "A" yellow green. Paint small country blue dots 1/8" (3 mm) apart on the letter "A."

7 Paint Christmas green medium dots 1/4" (6 mm) apart on the letters "D." Then paint 4 yellow green small dots around and slightly overlapping the Christmas green dots, as shown in the Step 7 illustration.

8 Follow Step 5 to paint the black stitch lines around the letters.

9 To finish each cup, air dry at least 7 days. Refer to the manufacturer's instructions to wash the cups.

Grandma's Photo Shirt

Even though Grandma already has everything, give her something she will cherish for her birthday—a gift you made from the heart! Transfer copies of your favorite photos to a shirt Grandmother will love to show off.

List of Materials

- White sweatshirt
- Photocopies of photographs, black and white or color
- Fabric transfer medium*
- 1" (2.5 cm) upper case calligraphy alphabet stencil*

- Air-soluble marking pen
- Fabric paints*: rose shimmer brush-on; dimensional: gold glitter; rose pearl; ice blue
- Paintbrushes: No. 4 fabric shader; 1" (2.5 cm) sponge

- Miscellaneous items: T-shirt board, plastic wrap, masking tape, wax paper, tracing paper, pencil, 4" x 5" (10 x 12.5 cm) cardboard, scissors, straight pins, toothpicks

*(See Sources on pg. 175 for purchasing information.)

1 Wash and dry the sweatshirt; do not use fabric softener.

2 Cover the T-shirt board with plastic wrap and insert it into the shirt. Smooth the shirt front over the board, pulling the excess fabric to the back; secure with masking tape. Cover the work area with wax paper.

3 Trace the pattern onto tracing paper and cut from cardboard to make a template. Use the template to cut photocopies into heart shapes.

4 Position the photos on the shirt front, leaving room for the lettering. Mark each area with straight pins.

5 Refer to the manufacturer's instructions to apply a thick coat of the transfer medium to the front of the photos with the sponge brush and to transfer the images to the marked areas on the shirt.

6 Use the stencil to trace the lettering onto the shirt front with the air-soluble pen. Paint the letters with rose shimmer paint using the shader brush, as shown in the Step 6 illustration. Let dry. Outline the letters with dimensional gold glitter paint.

7 Outline each heart with alternating dots of rose pearl and ice blue. Randomly paint hearts on the shirt front. To make a heart, make 2 paint dots side by side with a toothpick; then use the toothpick to pull the paint downward from each dot into a point. Squeeze a gold glitter dot below each heart. Let dry.

Heart
Cut 1 from cardboard
1 of 1

Say It With Dream Stones

Add a bit of poetry to a loved one's corner of the world with a collection of spicy clay "saying stones." Mix translucent polymer clay with assorted herbs and spices to create realistic-looking stones. Rubber stamp the stones with poetic messages or thoughts near and dear to his or her heart, then bake the clay to harden. They'll be such a hit you'll want to make several sets as birthday gifts.

List of Materials

- Translucent polymer clay, 2-oz. (50 g) block, 2
- Matte glaze
- Assorted herbs and spices: lemon pepper; lemon dill blend; Mexican chili powder; poppy seeds; poultry seasoning

- Rubber stamp sets: miniature upper and lower case alphabets; poetic words, your choice
- Black acrylic paint
- Paintbrushes: No. 1 liner; No. 10 flat

- Miscellaneous items: kitchen knife; cutting board; measuring spoons; disposable palette; water basin; foil-lined baking sheet; paper towels

1　Divide each clay block into quarters. Follow the manufacturer's instructions to knead each piece until pliable and roll into a ball.

2　To color the clay, refer to the Message/Color Guide. Roll each clay ball into a $^1/_2$ teaspoon (2 mL) or less of the indicated herb or seasoning and knead until well blended. When baked, the clay becomes more translucent. For marbled clay, blend 2 colored clay pieces together until just mixed.

3　Shape the clay pieces into smooth round and oval stones in assorted sizes, depending on the word you will stamp on stone. Press the top of each one with your fingers to slightly flatten.

4　Refer to the Message/Color Guide and the Step 4 illustration to press clean, uninked rubber stamps onto the surface of the clay stones, leaving their impressions. Use a word stamp or individual letters to spell a word on a stone, then group the stones to form phrases.

5　Refer to the manufacturer's instructions to bake the stones on a foil-lined baking sheet. Some cracks will appear after baking, adding realism to the stones. Let cool completely.

6　Use the liner brush and black to paint the words or use a fine-line black marker. Remove any excess paint with a damp cloth. Let dry. Use the flat brush to apply a coat of glaze to each stone. Let dry.

Message/Color Guide

Word	Herb/Spice
Love	Poppy seeds/Mexican chili powder marbled
Makes	Mexican chili powder
A	Poppy seeds
Garden	Lemon dill
Grow	Poppy seeds
Dance	Mexican chili powder
The	Lemon dill
Color	Poppy seeds
Of	Lemon dill/Mexican chili powder marbled
Life	Poultry seasoning

Leaf Quilt

Here is a quilt to "fall" in love with, every pun intended. With nine-patch blocks pieced in autumn's rich tones, strip borders and leaf appliqués, this design has a contemporary feel but looks very traditional. At 53" x 58" (134.5 x 147 cm), it will be a generous birthday gift for one you really love. Machine quilting and appliquéing makes it quicker to do than you would think.

List of Materials

- New Home/Janome Memory Craft 9000 sewing machine and Memory Card No. 10, or another machine

- 45" (115 cm) cotton print fabrics: brown, tan, 2 yd. (1.85 m) each; fall, 1 1/4 yd. (1.15 m); sage, 1/2 yd. (0.5 m); backing, 3 1/4 yd. (3.0 m)

- Cotton quilt batting, 54" x 60" (137 x 152.5 cm)

- Thread: machine embroidery, green; bobbin, to match backing

- 1/2" (1.3 cm) bias tape maker

- 6 mm twin needle

- Miscellaneous items: scissors, iron, straight pins, rotary cutter and mat, small sharp scissors

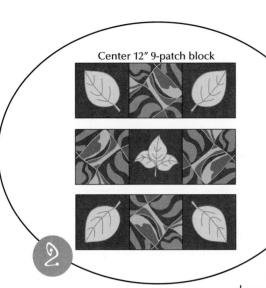

Center 12" 9-patch block

1 Cut the following fabric strips: brown, fall, 4¹/2" x 44" (11.5 x 112 cm), 1 each; fall, tan, 3" x 44" (7.5 x 112 cm), 5 each; brown, 3" x 44" (7.5 x 112 cm), 4; tan for binding, 4" x 44" (10 x 112 cm), 5; brown, 5" x 44" (12.5 x 112 cm), 6; tan, 8" x 44" (20.5 x 112 cm), 4; sage, 1" (2.5 cm) bias strips to make 4²/3 yd. (4.33 m) of bias tape.

2 Use ¹/4" (6 mm) seams, pressing seams to the darker fabric. Follow the machine manufacturer's instructions and the Step 2 illustration to construct a 12" (30.5 cm) 9-patch block for the quilt center from the 4¹/2" (11.5 cm) strips. If you don't have a New Home machine, purchase a leaf stencil, or draw freehand, cutting 4 individual leaves and a 3-part leaf from tan fabric. Appliqué leaves to the brown squares with a decorative stitch all around the edges and make leaf vein lines.

3 Refer to the photo and the Step 3 illustration to use 3" (7.5 cm) tan and fall strips to construct two 2x5-block strips alternating fabric squares. Sew these strips to opposite sides of the center 9-patch block. From the remaining 3" (7.5 cm) strips, sew six 7" (18 cm) 9-patch blocks and make 2 rows of 3 horizontal blocks; sew to top and bottom of center piece.

4 Sew border 3" (7.5 cm) brown strip to each side of patchwork center. Trim edges even. Repeat along top and bottom. Sew tan 8" (20.5 cm) border. Sew bias strips together to form 1 long strip. Use the bias tape maker to create a 4²/3 yd. (4.33 m) finished bias strip. With twin needle, sew bias strip to tan border as a winding vine. Trim at corners where leaf motifs will cover unfinished edges.

5 Set machine for Profession-Style embroidery and insert Memory Card No. 10. Place green embroidery thread in top needle and thread to match backing in bobbin. Refer to the photo and manufacturer's instructions to position fall fabric next to vine where leaf appliqués will be stitched. Using patterns No. 6 and 9, sew leaf designs randomly along vine and at corners. Repeat designs using tan fabric on brown squares of center 9-patch. If you do not have a New Home Machine, follow Step 2 to cut leaves from fall fabric and appliqué them around the vine.

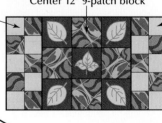

7" 9-patch blocks

Center 12" 9-patch block

Two 2x5-block strips

Two 2x5-block strips

6 Sew together short ends of three 5" (12.5 cm) brown strips to make 1 long strip. Cut in half. Repeat with other 3 strips. Refer to Step 4 to add final border to quilt. Sandwich batting between wrong sides of quilt top and backing; pin. Stitch-in-the-ditch using stitch Nos. 154, 155, 156 or 157 at seam lines; for non-New Home machines use a straight stitch.

7 Refer to Step 6 to sew binding strips together to be 3" (7.5 cm) longer than quilt perimeter. Fold strip in half lengthwise, wrong sides together. Match raw edges of binding and quilt; stitch. Turn binding to back of quilt and use stitch No. 27, or a blind appliqué, to finish binding hem.

Rustic Frame

This very special photo frame is made with materials gathered from your own back yard. Just think how special this birthday gift will be when it is handmade with love. Naturally, the recipient will be pleased!

List of Materials

- Tree bark
- Utility knife
- Photograph or artwork
- Glass, cut to fit photograph or artwork
- Foam board, 3/8" (1 cm) thick
- Hot glue gun and glue sticks

- Mat board
- Embellishments, such as lichens or moss, if desired
- Self-adhesive hanger, if desired
- Miscellaneous items: wood chisel or putty knife, iron, scrap wood boards, plastic bag

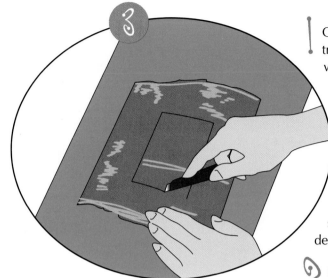

Collect loose tree bark from firewood or fallen trees. If the bark is not loose, cut it lengthwise with a utility knife and pry the bark away from the wood with a wood chisel or putty knife. Scrape off any excess fibrous material from the back of the bark. Flatten slightly curled bark by steaming it with an iron and pressing it between two boards until dry. Moisten severely curled bark and seal it in a plastic bag until it is pliable enough to press flat. To cut the bark to the desired size, use a utility knife or tear the bark to the desired size and shape.

2. Cut 3 spacers from foam board, 1/2" (1.3 cm) wide, with the length of 1 spacer equal to the length of the lower edge of the glass and the length of the remaining 2 spacers equal to the length of the sides of the glass. Cut a mat board backing 1" (2.5 cm) longer than the sides of the glass and 1 3/4" (4.5 cm) wider than the upper and lower edges of the glass. Cut a mat board shim the same size as the photograph.

3. Place the bark frame facedown on work surface. Mark opening in desired location on the back of the frame, with measurements 1/2" (1.3 cm) narrower and shorter than the width and length of the glass and photograph. Cut opening, using utility knife, as shown in the Step 3 illustration.

4. Glue foam board spacer for lower edge of opening to back of frame, using hot glue gun and centering spacer 1/4" (6 mm) below opening. Glue the foam board spacers for the sides 3/8" (1 cm) beyond opening edges.

5. See the Step 5 illustration to hot-glue the mat board backing over spacers; lower and side edges of the backing will extend 1/4" (6 mm) beyond spacers. Attach a self-adhesive hanger, if desired.

6. Place the photograph face down on glass; place mat board shim over the photograph; slide into place between the backing and the frame opening. Embellish with lichens or moss, if desired, gluing them to bark.

Herbal Kitchen Wreath

Pay your respects to the birthday man or woman with a hand-made wreath that will allow the fragrance of herbs to be enjoyed all year round. In addition, it will make a welcoming accent in any entryway, kitchen or family room. If the guest of honor is an avid gardener or gourmet cook, this wreath will be even more special. The cook can actually use the herbs, making it ever-so-practical, and if you could sneak items from the gardener's own harvest to put on the wreath, think how proud he or she will be to see it so beautifully displayed.

List of materials

- 16" (40.5 cm) Spanish moss wreath, one
- 2¹/₂" to 3" (6.5 to 7.5 cm) chili peppers, 100
- Garlic chives with 4" (10 cm) heads, five
- Lemon mint with 1" (2.5 cm) heads, 30
- Garlic bulbs, 15
- 1¹/₄" (3.2 cm) wire-edge copper mesh ribbon, 2 yd. (1.85 m)
- Natural raffia strands, 2 yd. (1.85 m) lengths, three or four
- 12" (30.5 cm) of craft wire
- Floral pins
- Glue
- Miscellaneous items: scissors, ruler

1 | If you cannot find a Spanish moss wreath, purchase a 16" (40.5 cm) straw wreath and Spanish moss. Hot-glue the moss in a layer all around the front and side edges of the wreath, tucking the moss around to the back side.

2 | Use floral pins to secure 5 clusters, each with 20 chili peppers, equally spaced around the wreath.

3 | Cut the stems of the garlic chives 1½" (3.8 cm) long. Pin 1 garlic chive head near the base of each chili pepper cluster.

4 | Glue 3 garlic bulbs near the base of each chili pepper cluster, as shown in the Step 4 illlustration.

5 | Cut the stems of the lemon mint flowers 2" (5 cm) long and randomly glue them between the garlic chives and chili peppers.

6 | Loosely drape and pin the copper mesh ribbon, then the raffia between the dried materials. Trim away the excess.

7 | Attach wire to the back of the wreath for a wreath hanger.

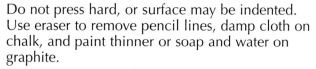

Painting

General Instructions

1. Sanding: Many projects are done on wood, and so must be sanded. If painting on a nonwood surface, make sure it is clean and dry. Begin the process with coarse-grit sandpaper, and end with finer grits. A 150-grit sandpaper will put finish smoothness on surfaces, such as preparing for staining or sanding. A 220-grit extra-fine sandpaper is good for smoothing stained or painted wood before varnishing, or between coats. Use a tack cloth—a treated, sticky cheesecloth—to lightly remove sanding dust after each step. Don't rub over the surface or you will leave a sticky residue on the wood. Wood files, sanding blocks and emery boards can be used to sand hard-to-reach places and curves.

2. Transferring: Place pattern on surface or wood, following direction for grainline. For pattern outlines, such as for cutting your own pieces, use a pencil to trace around pattern piece onto wood. Trace lightly, so wood is not indented. To transfer detail lines, you can use pencil, chalk, transfer paper or graphite paper. Ink beads over many waxed transfer papers, so if you plan to use fine-line permanent-ink markers for detail lines, be sure to use graphite or wax-free transfer paper. Transfer as few lines as possible, painting freehand instead.

Do not press hard, or surface may be indented. Use eraser to remove pencil lines, damp cloth on chalk, and paint thinner or soap and water on graphite.

To use pencil or chalk, rub the wrong side of traced pattern. Shake off any loose lead; lay pattern penciled or chalk-side down on wood, and retrace pattern with a pencil or stylus.

To use transfer or graphite paper, place paper face-down on wood, then place pattern on top. Lightly trace over pattern lines. Lay a piece of wax paper on top of pattern to be traced. This protects your original traced pattern and also lets you see what you have traced.

3. Brushes: The size should always correspond in size to the area being painted, preferably with the largest brush that will fit the design area. The brush should also reflect the technique being done, which is usually suggested in craft project directions.

4. Extender: Acrylic extender is a medium to add to acrylic paints to increase their open time. Open time refers to the amount of time in which you can mix and blend the paints before they begin to dry. Those familiar with oil paints are most concerned with this, or if you are doing very complex designs with a great deal of shading.

Painting Techniques

Basecoating:

Applying the first coat of paint to a prepared surface, usually covering the surface and all edges in entirety. Sometimes two coats of paint are recommended. Basecoating is usually done with a flat or sponge brush.

Dots:

Dots can be made by dipping the end of the paintbrush or stylus or even a toothpick in paint and then touching it gently on the painted surface. This technique can create perfect eyes or dots better than any brush tip.

Double Loading:

This is the same as side loading, except two colors are loaded, one on each side of the brush. The colors gradually blend into one another in the middle of the brush.

Dots

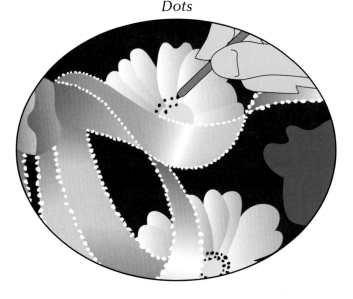

Dry-Brushing:

This technique is used to achieve a soft or aged look; many times it is used to blush cheeks. Dip dry brush tips in a small amount of paint (undiluted for heavy coverage and diluted for transparent coverage). Wipe on paper towel until almost no paint is left. Then gently brush on the surface.

Highlighting:

Highlighting is the reverse of shading, causing an area to be more prominent. Thus a lighter color, such as white, is often loaded on a flat brush and used for highlighting. Highlighting is also sometimes done with a liner brush, by painting a straight line with a light color over an area to give a dimensional appearance.

Loading, Side Loading or Floating Color:

Loading or floating is usually done with a flat or shader brush. Dip or load brush in water; then lightly blot on paper towel to release some moisture. Load or pull one side of the brush through paint. Blend paint on a mixing surface so the color begins to move across the bristles, and is dark on one edge, but light on the other. Make sure to get the paint well blended before actually painting on the surface. Another method is to thin the paint (see next page) and mix it well. Load the paint by dipping one corner in and blending well on a mixing surface, as above.

Stippling (or Pouncing):

This is a stenciling technique, and is very similar to dry-brushing, except it gives a more fuzzy or textured look. Stencil, fabric or stippler brushes may be used, or any old scruffy brush. Dip just brush tips in a small amount of paint; then blot on paper towel until brush is almost dry. Apply the paint to the surface by pouncing up and down with the bristle tips until desired coverage is achieved.

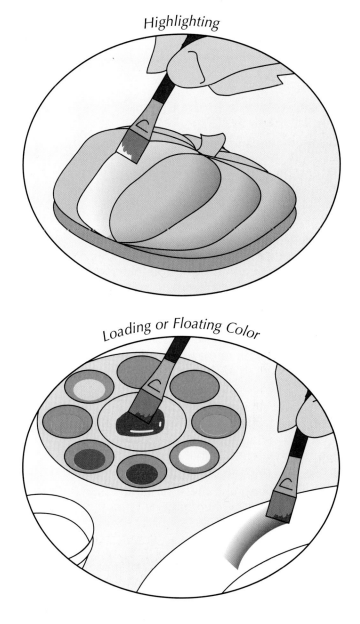

Highlighting

Loading or Floating Color

(continued)

Painting Techniques *(continued)*

Shading:

Shading is done with a color darker than the main color, making an area recede into the background. It is frequently used on edges of designs and done with the side load or floating technique. On an orange background, the brush is loaded with rust, and pulled along the edge, with the paint edge of brush where color is to be darkest.

Strokes—Comma Stroke, C-Stroke and S-Stroke:

Make the thin and thick lines by adjusting the pressure on the brush and letting the brush hairs pull together to create the "tails" at the beginning and end of the strokes. Wipe and reload the brush for every stroke. Clean the brush occasionally with water, wipe dry, and reload paint. Practice several times before actually painting the object, always pulling the brush toward you. You will find that you make one of the strokes, left or right, better than the other.

- *Comma Stroke:* Begin at the head by pressing down on the brush for a wide line. While curving around to make the comma, release the pressure to make the thin tail before lifting off the brush.

- *C-Stroke:* With the brush tip, pull a thin line, then press down on the brush for a wide line. While curving around to make the C, pull another thin line before lifting off the brush.

- *S-Stroke:* With the brush tip, pull a thin line. Turn the brush and press for a wide line, then turn and pull another thin line before lifting off the brush.

Thinning:

Add drops of water and mix until the paint is of an ink-like consistency. Sometimes a specific mix of water and paint is requested.

Wash:

Dilute the paint with five parts water to one part paint (or whatever proportion is requested) and mix well. Load the brush, and blot excess paint on brush onto a paper towel. Fill in the area to be painted, giving transparent coverage. A wash can also be used for shading or highlighting large areas.

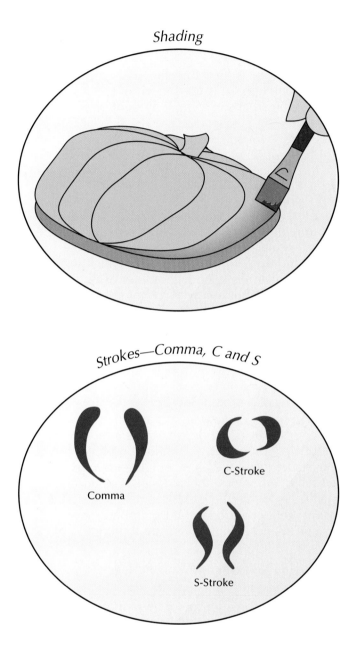

Shading

Strokes—Comma, C and S

Comma

C-Stroke

S-Stroke

Embroidery

Ribbon Embroidery

Backstitch

Up at 1, down at 2, up at 3, down at 1, stitching back to meet previous stitch.

Blanket Stitch

Down at 1, up at 2 with thread below needle; pull through.

Blanket Stitch Corner 1

Make a diagonal blanket stitch at 1. Tack stitch on wrong side at corner, leaving loop. Insert needle through loop at 2; pull taut. Continue stitching.

Blanket Stitch Corner 2

To work corner, use same center hole to work stitches 1, 2, and 3.

French Knot

Up at 1, wrap thread specified number of times around needle, down near 1.

Lazy Daisy

Up at 1, make loop, down at 1. Up at 2, down at 3 to tack loop.

Running Stitch

Up at odd, down at even numbers for specified length.

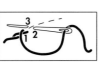

Satin Stitch

Up at 1, down at 2, up at 3, working parallel stitches.

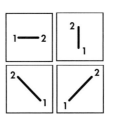

Stem Stitch

Up at 1, down at 2, up at 3, keeping thread to left of needle and working slightly slanted stitches along the line of design.

Straight Stitch

Work stitches for specified length.

French Knot

Up at 1, wrap ribbon once around needle, down near 1.

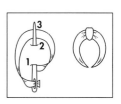

Lazy Daisy

Up at 1, holding ribbon flat with thumb. Make loop, down near 1. Up at 2, make small anchor stitch over ribbon at 3.

Needle Lock

To lock ribbon on needle, insert threaded needle 1/2" (1.3 cm) from end of ribbon. Pull on opposite end to lock.

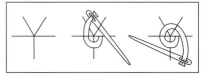

Spider Web Rose

With floss, stitch 5 spokes for the anchor. With ribbon, come up in center and work in an over and under pattern around spokes, keeping ribbon loose and letting it twist. Fill in to cover spokes.

Stem Stitch

Up at 1, down at 2, up at 3, keeping ribbon to left of needle and working slightly slanted stitches along the line of design.

Cross-Stitch

General Instructions

1. Overcast the edges to prevent raveling. Fold the fabric in half vertically and horizontally to find the center, and mark it with a temporary stitch. If desired, place the fabric in an embroidery hoop. Find the center of the design by following arrows on the Chart. Count up and over to the top left stitch or specified point and begin stitching.

2. Each square on a Cross-Stitch Chart represents one square of evenweave fabric, unless otherwise indicated. Symbols correspond to the colors given in the Color Key.

3. Cut floss into 18" (46 cm) lengths. Separate the strands and use the number specified in the project. Stitching tends to twist the floss; allow the needle to hang free from your work to untwist it from time to time.

4. To begin, do not knot the floss, but hold a tail on the back of the work until anchored by the first few stitches. To carry the floss across the back to another area to be stitched, weave the floss under previously worked stitches to new area, but do not carry the floss more than three or four stitches. To end the floss, run it under several stitches on the back, and cut it. Do not use knots.

5. Work all cross-stitches first, then any additional stitches, including backstitches. Work in horizontal rows wherever possible. To make vertical stitches, complete each cross-stitch before moving to the next one.

6. When stitching is completed, wash the fabric in warm sudsy water if needed. Roll it in a terry-cloth towel to remove excess moisture. Press it facedown on another terry-cloth towel to dry.

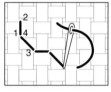

Backstitch
Up at 1, down at 2, up at 3, down at 4, stitching back to meet prior stitch.

Cross-Stitch
Work first half of each stitch left to right; complete each stitch right to left.

French Knot
Up at 1, wrap thread indicated number of times around needle, down at 1.

Perforated Plastic

General Instructions

1. To stitch perforated plastic, count squares, not holes. Each square is surrounded by 4 holes. On the stitch chart, each square represents one 4-hole square wherein a stitch is made.

2. To cut perforated plastic, count the squares on the stitch chart and cut the canvas accordingly, cutting down the middle of a row of holes. Follow the bold outlines. Use a craft knife to cut small areas.

3. To stitch, do not knot the yarn or floss, but hold a tail in back and anchor with the first few stitches. To end yarn or floss, weave tail under stitches on back; then cut it. Do not stitch over edge bars.

4. When finished stitching individual pieces, finish edges and join pieces as specified with an overcast stitch.

5. Cut floss into 18" (46 cm) lengths. Separate the strands and use the number specified in the project. Stitching tends to twist the floss; allow the needle to hang free from your work to untwist it from time to time.

Cross-Stitch
Work first half of each stitch left to right; complete each stitch right to left.

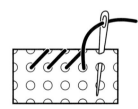

Overcast
Use a whipping motion over outer edges.

Crochet

Abbreviations

beg	Beginning
bet	Between
ch	Chain
dc	Double Crochet
lp(s)	Loop(s)
rem	Remaining
rep	Repeat
rnd(s)	Round(s)
sc	Single Crochet
sk	Skip
sl st	Slip Stitch
sp(s)	Space(s)
st(s)	Stitch(es)
tog	Together
tr	Treble Crochet
yo	Yarn Over
*	Repeat following instructions a given number of times

Beginning Slip Knot

Begin with a slip knot on hook about 6″ (15 cm) from end of yarn. Insert hook through loop; pull to tighten.

Chain Stitch (ch)

Yarn over, draw yarn through loop on hook to form new loop.

Double Crochet (dc)

1. For first row, yarn over, insert hook into 4th chain from hook. Yarn over; draw through 2 loops on hook.

2. Yarn over, and pull yarn through last 2 loops on hook.

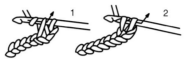

Forming Ring with a Slip Stitch

1. Insert hook in first chain.

2. Yarn over, and pull through all loops on hook.

Single Crochet (sc)

1. For first row, insert hook into second chain from hook, and draw up a loop.

2. Yarn over, and draw through both loops on hook.

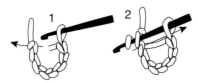

Slip Stitch (sl st)

Insert hook in stitch, yarn over, and draw through both loops on hook.

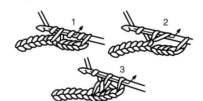

Treble Crochet (tr)

For first row yarn over 2 times; insert hook into 5th chain from hook and draw up loop.

1. Yarn over and pull through first 2 loops on hook.

2. Yarn over and pull through 2 loops on hook.

3. Yarn over and pull through last 2 loops on hook.

Yo Yos

1. Cut circles from assorted fabrics, making their diameters twice the desired size. For example, if you need a finished 1″ (2.5 cm) yo yo, cut a circle with a 2″ (5 cm) diameter.

2. Sew running stitches by hand or long machine stitches for gathering all around the edge that are 1/4″ (6 mm) in. Do not knot the ends; leave long thread tails.

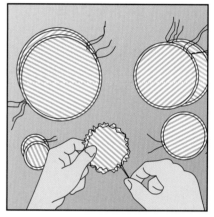

3. See the illustration to evenly pull threads tight, gathering the fabric circle tightly in the center to make a yo yo. Turn the circle right side out.

4. Flatten and shape the yo yo. Knot threads to hold yo yo in place, and tuck the tails into the center.

Sampler Stitch Chart 2 of 2

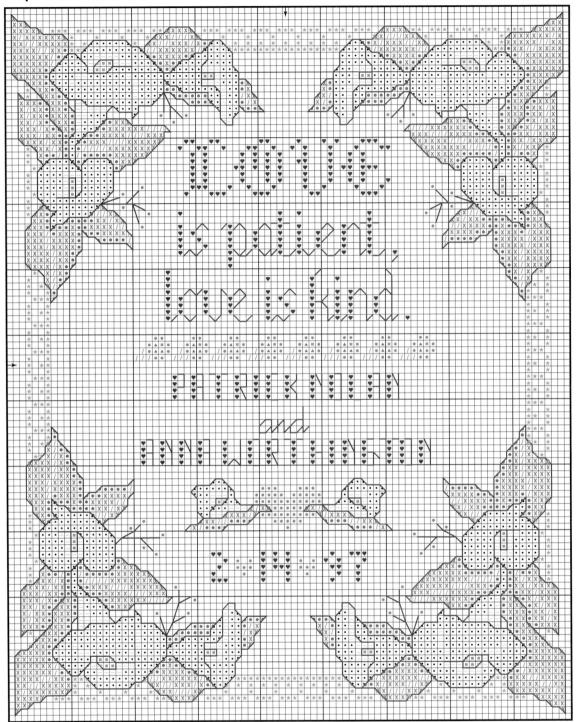

Color/Stitch Key

Symbol	Anchor #	Color	Symbol	Anchor #	Color
•	01	Snow White	▪	311	Vy. Lt. Tangerine
•	06	Vy. Lt. Salmon	▲	1009	Vy. Lt. Copper
/	206	Lt. Spruce	—	1031	Ultra Lt. Antique Blue
x	208	Med. Lt. Spruce	♥	1035	Dk. Antique Blue
●	217	Med. Dk. Juniper	★	002HL	Metallic Gold Braid Backstitches

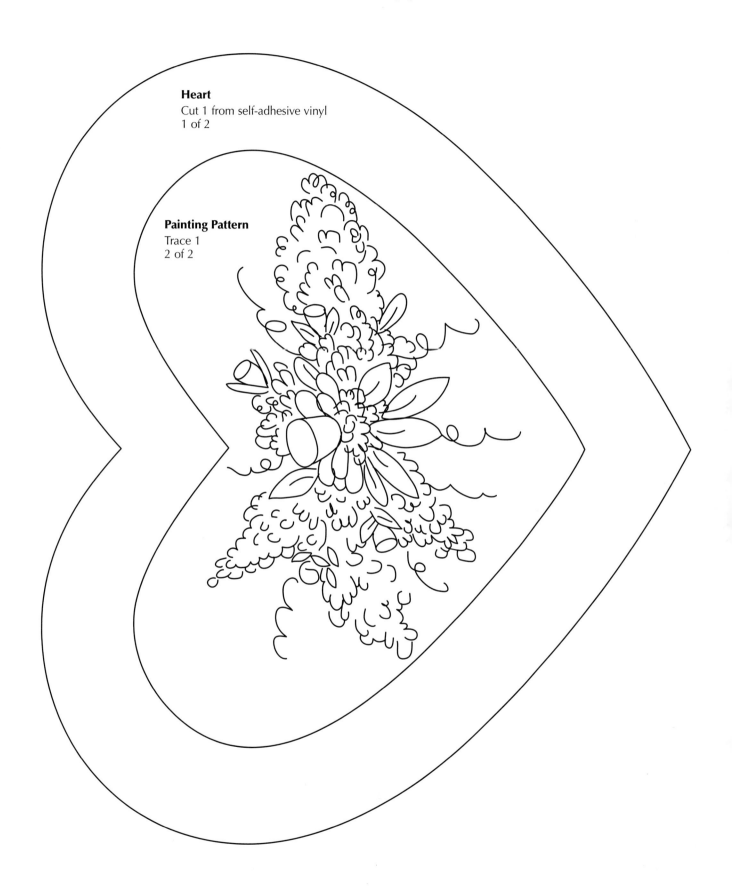

Heart
Cut 1 from self-adhesive vinyl
1 of 2

Painting Pattern
Trace 1
2 of 2

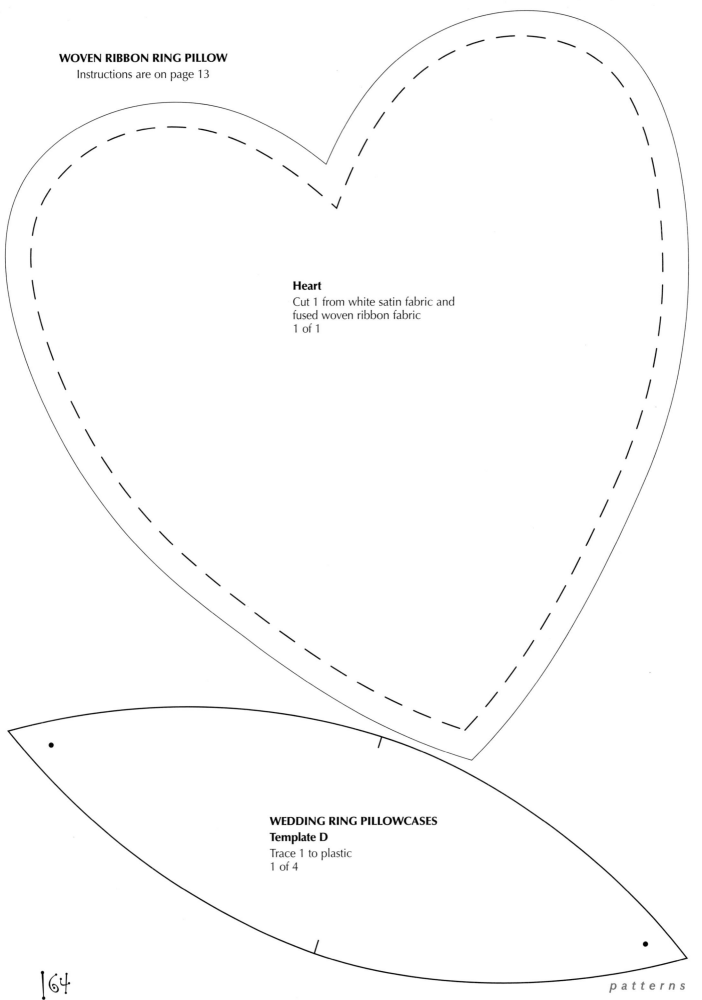

Heart
Cut 1 from white satin fabric and
fused woven ribbon fabric
1 of 1

WEDDING RING PILLOWCASES
Template D
Trace 1 to plastic
1 of 4

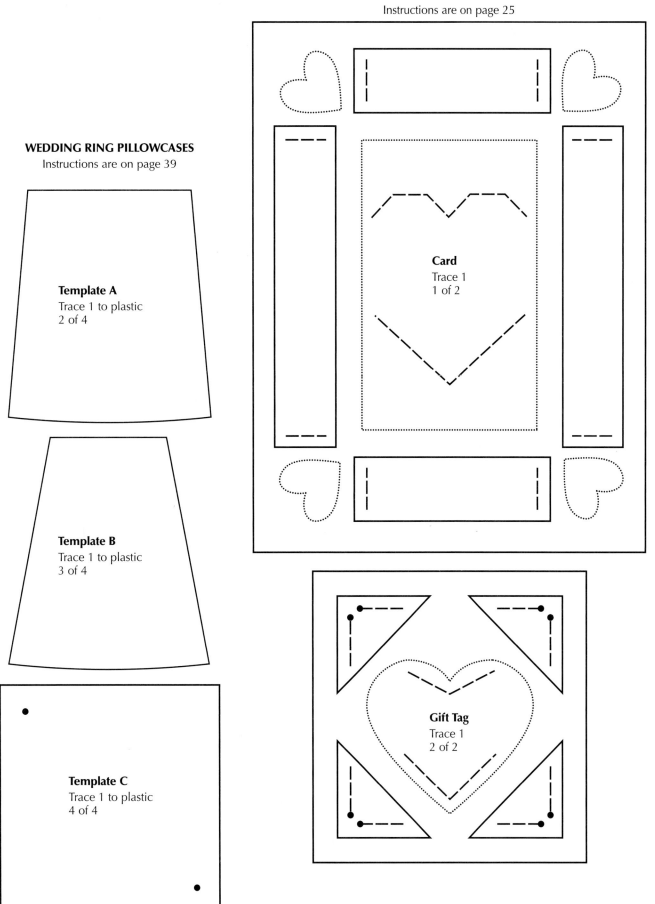

WEDDING RING PILLOWCASES
Instructions are on page 39

Template A
Trace 1 to plastic
2 of 4

Template B
Trace 1 to plastic
3 of 4

Template C
Trace 1 to plastic
4 of 4

Card
Trace 1
1 of 2

Gift Tag
Trace 1
2 of 2

patterns

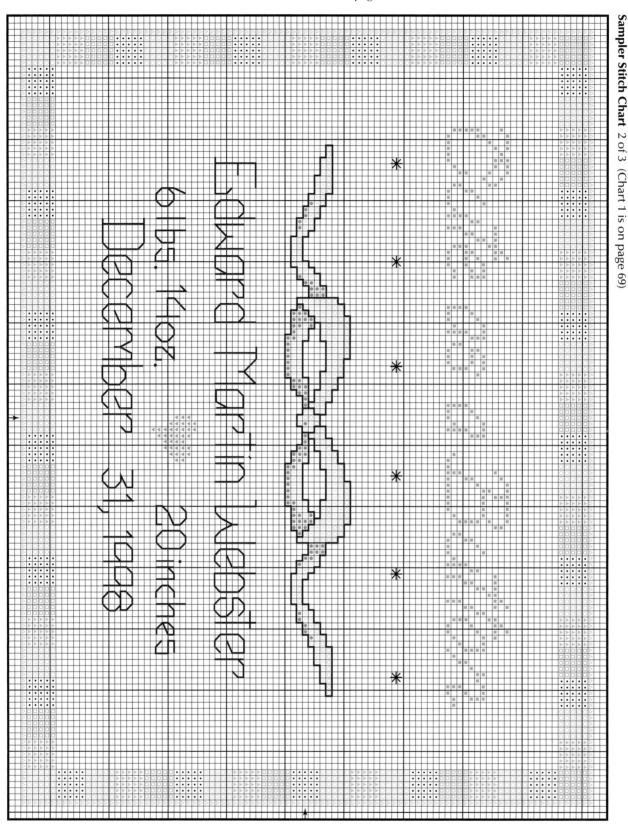

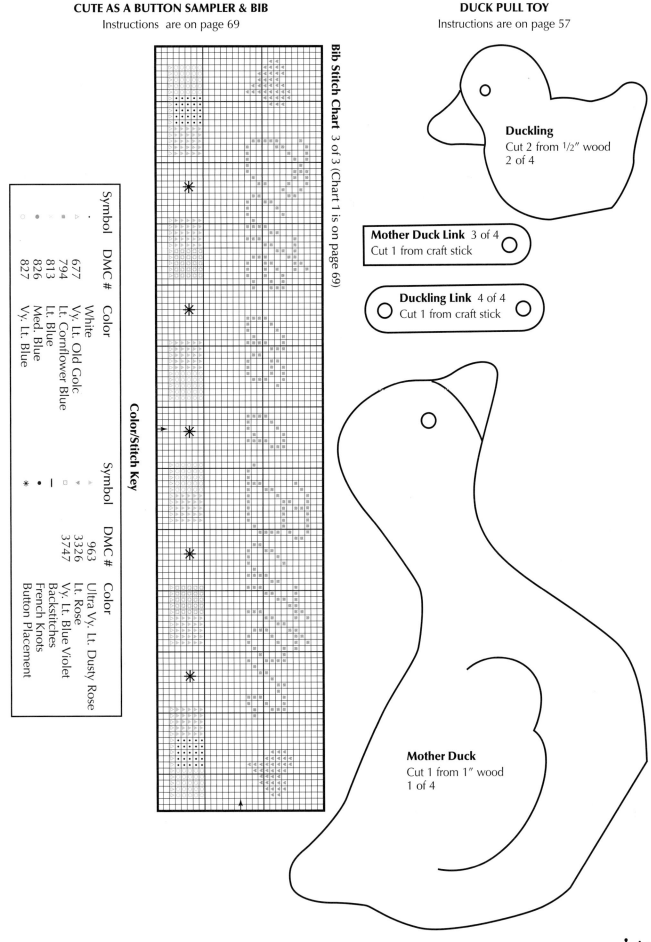

Bib Stitch Chart 3 of 3 (Chart 1 is on page 69)

Color/Stitch Key

Symbol	DMC #	Color
○	677	White
●	794	Vy. Lt. Old Gold
▷	813	Lt. Cornflower Blue
▪	826	Lt. Blue
×		Med. Blue
○	827	Vy. Lt. Blue

Symbol	DMC #	Color
▶	963	Ultra Vy. Lt. Dusty Rose
◀	3326	Lt. Rose
□	3747	Vy. Lt. Blue Violet
—		Backstitches
●		French Knots
✳		Button Placement

Duckling
Cut 2 from 1/2" wood
2 of 4

Mother Duck Link 3 of 4
Cut 1 from craft stick

Duckling Link 4 of 4
Cut 1 from craft stick

Mother Duck
Cut 1 from 1" wood
1 of 4

Engine Front Stitch Chart 2 of 7
Cut 1 from perforated plastic

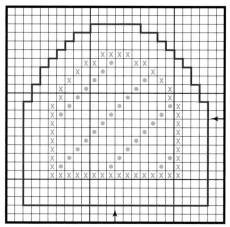

Engine Side Stitch Chart 1 of 7
Cut 1 from perforated plastic

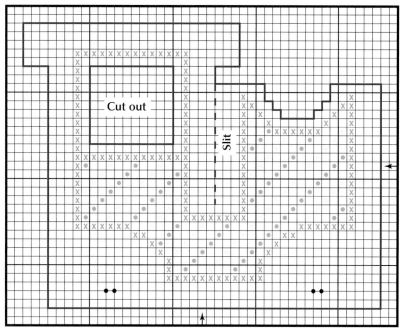

Engine Side Stitch Chart 3 of 7
Cut 1 from perforated plastic

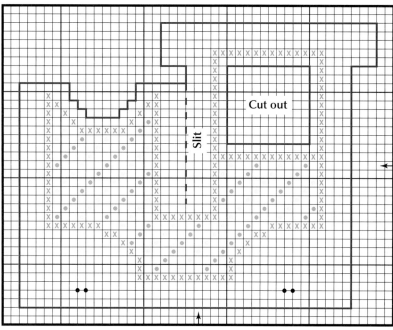

Boxcar Side Stitch Chart 4 of 7
Cut 2 from perforated plastic

Caboose Side Stitch Chart 5 of 7

Cut 2 from perforated plastic

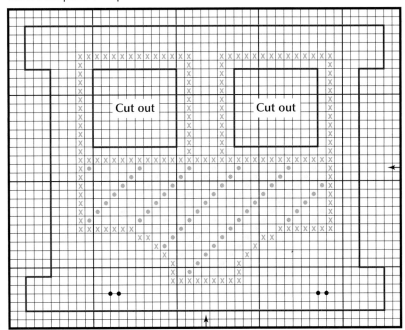

Color Key

Symbol	Anchor #	Color
●	008	Coral
x	185	Aqua
	288	Yellow
● ●		Button Placement

Smoke Stack Stitch Chart 6 of 7

Cut 1 from perforated plastic

Cab Front Stitch Chart 7 of 7

Cut 1 from perforated plastic

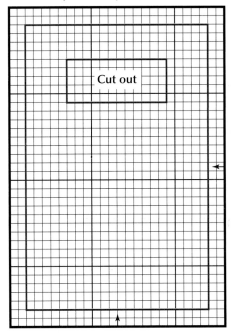

Hooded Towel Stitch Chart 2 of 2

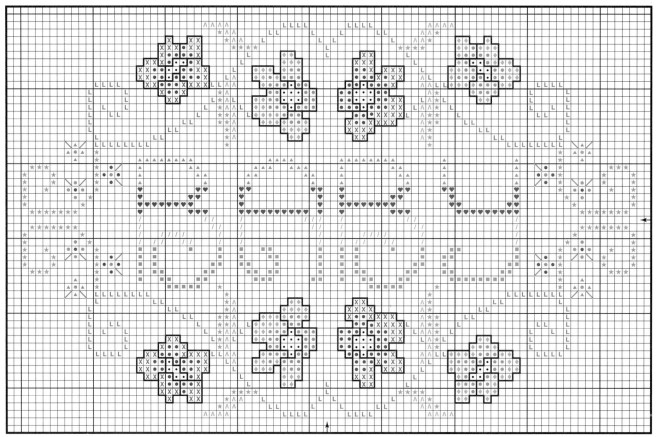

Baby Girl Color/Stitch Key

Symbol	Anchor #	Color
•	01	White
▲	25	Lt. Carnation
■	69	Med. Raspberry
♥	76	Med. Antique Rose
/	77	Med. Dk. Antique Rose
X	144	Vy. Lt. Delft Blue
●	145	Lt. Delft Blue
∧	203	Lt. Mint Green
L	204	Med. Mint Green
★	206	Lt. Spruce
●	300	Lt. Citrus
◆	386	Vy. Lt. Citrus
–	212	Dk. Spruce Straight Stitch Flower Leaves
—	162	Med. Dk. Sapphire Backstitches

Baby Boy Color/Stitch Key

Symbol	Anchor #	Color
•	01	White
X	25	Lt. Carnation
●	76	Med. Antique Rose
▲	144	Vy. Lt. Delft Blue
♥	145	Lt. Delft Blue
∧	203	Lt. Mint Green
L	204	Med. Mint Green
★	206	Lt. Spruce
●	300	Lt. Citrus
◆	386	Vy. Lt. Citrus
/	977	Med. Sea Blue
■	978	Med. Dk. Sea Blue
–	212	Dk. Spruce Straight Stitch Flower Leaves
—	69	Med. Raspberry Backstitches

TUTTI FRUTTI BEVERAGE SET

Instructions are on page 95

Cut 1 each from compressed sponge sheet

Square
1 of 4

Fruit Slice Section
2 of 4

Fruit Slice Center
3 of 4

Fruit Slice
4 of 4

HATS OFF TO GRADS

Instructions are on page 93

Hat D
Cut 2 from fused lamé
1 of 4

Hat A
Cut 4 from fused lamé
2 of 4

Hat C
Cut 2 from fused lamé
3 of 4

Hat B
Cut 3 from fused lamé
4 of 4

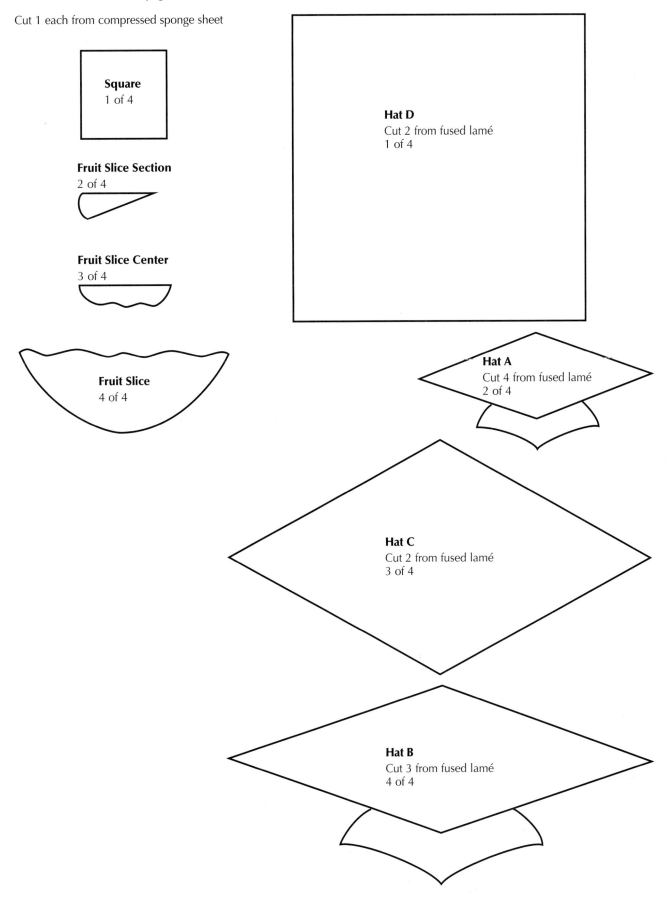

ABC Pincushion Stitch Chart 1 of 2

Sewing Pincushion Stitch Chart 2 of 2

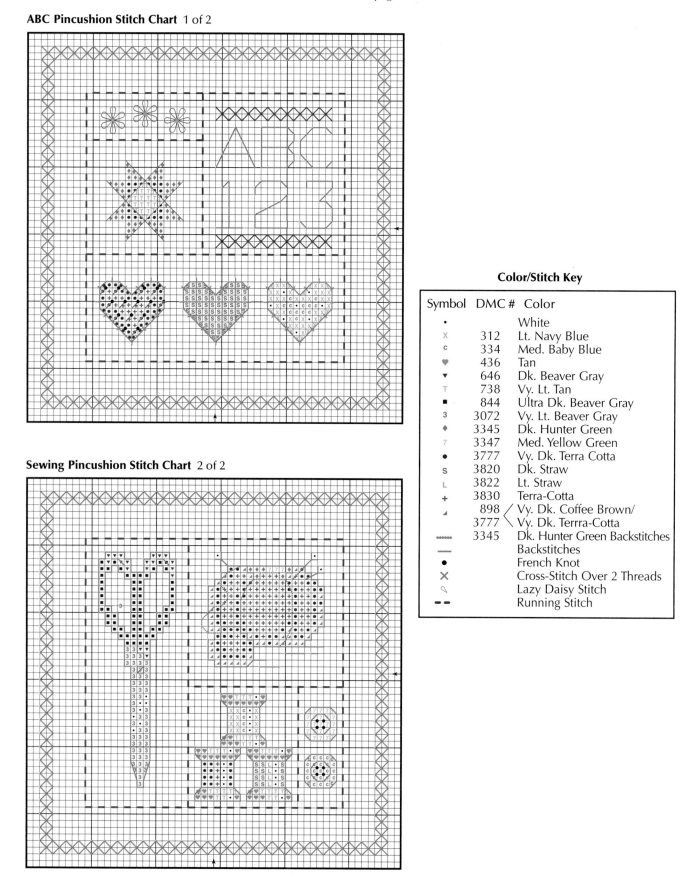

Color/Stitch Key

Symbol	DMC #	Color
•		White
X	312	Lt. Navy Blue
c	334	Med. Baby Blue
♥	436	Tan
▼	646	Dk. Beaver Gray
T	738	Vy. Lt. Tan
■	844	Ultra Dk. Beaver Gray
3	3072	Vy. Lt. Beaver Gray
◆	3345	Dk. Hunter Green
7	3347	Med. Yellow Green
●	3777	Vy. Dk. Terra Cotta
S	3820	Dk. Straw
L	3822	Lt. Straw
+	3830	Terra-Cotta
◢	898 ⟨	Vy. Dk. Coffee Brown/
	3777 ⟨	Vy. Dk. Terrra-Cotta
⠶⠶⠶⠶	3345	Dk. Hunter Green Backstitches
—		Backstitches
●		French Knot
X		Cross-Stitch Over 2 Threads
⟍		Lazy Daisy Stitch
– –		Running Stitch

Banner
Cut 1 from card stock
1 of 6

Pinwheel
Cut 1 from magazine
paper square
2 of 6

Star
Cut 5 from
watercolor paper
3 of 6

Face Pattern
4 of 6

Kite
Cut 2 from card stock
6 of 6

Wings
Cut 1 from watercolor paper
5 of 6

GONE FISHING WALL QUILT
Instructions are on page 111

Lettering
Trace 1
1 of 4

GONE
FISHING

Fish
Cut 3 from fused dark fabric
2 of 4

Upper Left Fish
Trace 1
3 of 4

Lower Right Fish
Trace 1
4 of 4

Graphic Tape Placement Guide
1 of 1

1/32" Blue

1/16" Blue

1/8" Red

1/8" Red

1/32" Blue

1/16" Yellow

1/8" Red

1/32" Blue

1/32" Blue

1/16" Blue

1/16" Blue

1/8" Red

1/16" Blue

1/16" Yellow

1/32" Red

FLORAL TREASURE BOX
Instructions are on page 137

Trace 1 of each flower painting pattern

Pansy
1 of 4

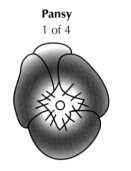

Daisy
2 of 4

Tulip
3 of 4

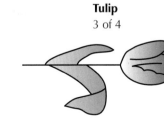

Roses
4 of 4

Sources

Most of these items are available at your local craft retail stores. If you are having difficulties locating items, or live far from a retail store, please reference the sources listed below.

Page 18, Toasting Glasses

- EtchAll® Etching Creme provided by B & B Products, Inc., 877-262-3824; www.etchall.com.
- Plaid® Simply® Laser Roses Stencil #28032 and Fun to Paint™ Tip-Pen Craft Tip Set #50136 provided by Plaid® Enterprises, Inc., 800-842-4197; www.plaidonline.com.

Page 28, Soothing Scents Bath Oil

- Oils and other bath product ingredients are available from Victorian Essences, 888-446-5455; www.Victorian-Essence.com.

Page 50, Baby Bathtime

- Daniel Enterprises Crafter's Pride hooded baby towel, burp cloth and bath mitt are available from Stitch and Frame Shop, 800-636-6341. Colors and trims may vary from those featured in the photo.

Page 80, Tote/Diaper Bag

- Memory Book Tote #2649-NAT provided by BagWorks™, Inc., 800-365-7423; www.bagworks.com.
- Rubber Stampede Decorative™ Stamping Paint: Ivory #65019; White #65036; Lavender #65022; Jade Green #65020; Bittersweet Orange #65003; Straw #65028; Indiana Rose #65018; Denim Blue #65011; Blue Jay #65005; Fuchsia #65013; and Stamps: Lamb #72014; Chick #72013; Bunny #72012 (all 3 animals Nursery Animals Kit #73001); Whimsical Butterfly #72060, Alphabet Kit #79001; and Applicator Sponges #67002 provided by Rubber Stampede, 800-NEATFUN; www.rubberstampede.com.

Page 86, Rubber Stamp Congrats for Grads

- Stamp Affair rubber stamps Congratulations (X648), star (S432); pigment ink pads opaque gold (OP102), opaque black (OP101); tangerine embossing pen (E1261); embossing powders gold (EP101), sparkle rainbow (EP117); and embossing gun (E1300-300) are available from home distributors at 800-4INKPAD.

Page 96, Painted Popcorn Keeper

- Popcorn keeper (200-0166) is available from Viking Woodcrafts, 800-328-0116.

Page 112, Rainbow Trout Clock

- DMC® embroidery floss was used. The desk clock (48021) is from Sudberry House, 860-739-6951.

Page 118, Springtime Mosaic Planter

- Window Box (62519) by Walnut Hollow, 800-950-5101.
- Plaid® Faster Plaster!™ Beginner Kits (67101 and 67105) Shake & Pour bottle, pastel paint set and glaze, Apple Barrel® Indoor/Outdoor Gloss Paint, Make-It Mosaics™ Bag o' Chips ceramic tiles, tile nippers, tile adhesive, white tile grout and tile sealer and painter's tape all available from Plaid® Enterprises, Inc., 800-842-4197; www.plaidonline.com.

Page 136, Floral Treasure Box

- Jewelry cabinet (813) is available from Wayne's Woodenware, 800-840-1497.

Page 138, Fabulous Floral Soaps

- Soaps, fragrance oils, soap molds and other ingredients are available from Victorian Essences, 888-446-5455; VicEss@aol.com.

Page 146, Grandma's Photo Shirt

- Picture This™ Transfer Medium, Simply® Stencil (28547) and Fashion Fabric paints are available from Plaid® Enterprises Inc., 800-842-4197; www.plaidonline.com.

Contributors

Thanks to the following manufacturers for donating these craft projects for publication purposes.

Page 12, Woven Ribbon Ring Pillow
- Provided by C. M. Offray &. Son; their ribbons were used.

Page 20, Cross-Stitch Album Cover
- Provided by Coats and Clark; their instant Stick and Hold™ sheet adhesive and Anchor® embroidery floss was used.

Page 22, Romantic Hurricane Globe
- Provided by Plaid® Enterprises Inc.; their FolkArt® glass and tile medium and acrylic paints were used.

Page 30, Delft Blues Embroidered Table Linens
- Provided by DMC®; their embroidery floss was used.

Page 34, Mosaic Trivet & Coasters
- Provided by Plaid® Enterprises, Inc.; their Faster Plaster™, Make-It Mosaics™ surface templates, tiles, marbles, tile nippers, tile adhesive and grout, and Apple Barrel® acrylic gloss enamel paint were used.

Page 52, Rainbow of Bunnies Bib
- Provided by DMC®; their embroidery floss was used.

Page 62, Summertime Crocheted Booties
- Provided by DMC®; their pearl cotton was used.

Page 68, Cute as a Button Sampler & Bib
- Provided by DMC®; their embroidery floss was used.

Page 94, Tutti-Frutti Beverage Set
- Provided by Delta; their CeramDecor™ Air Dry PermEnamel™ Surface Cleaner & Conditioner, paints and glaze were used.

Page 100, Collaged CD Holder
- Plaid® Enterprises; Inc. Mod Podge® was provided and used.

Page 150, Leaf Quilt
- Provided by Janome; their New Home embroidery and bobbin threads were used.